Who Said I Can't?

Roslyn Charnock

Australia

Copyright © 2022 by Roslyn Charnock.

All rights reserved. No part of this publication may be reproduced, distributed or transmitted in any form or by any means, including photocopying, recording, or other electronic or mechanical methods, without the prior written permission of the publisher, except in the case of brief quotations embodied in critical reviews and certain other noncommercial uses permitted by copyright law. For permission requests, write to the publisher, addressed "Attention: Permissions Coordinator," at the address below.

Roslyn Charnock C/- Intertype Publish and Print
Unit 45, 125 Highbury Road
BURWOOD VIC 3125
www.intertype.com.au

Ordering Information:
Quantity sales. Special discounts are available on quantity purchases by corporations, associations, and others. For details, contact the "Special Sales Department" at the address above.

Who Said I Can't/ Roslyn Charnock. —1st ed.
ISBN 978-0-6455754-1-5

Contents

Dedication 3

Introduction 5

How the family started 11

The School Years 23

Growing Up 35

Incidents 53

Holidays 67

Parties 73

Love Struck 83

Vulnerabilities 89

Post Script 106

Dedication

I want to dedicate this book to my loving family who have endured life's bumpy roads, the shortage of a parent handbook with instructions for me to avoid my mistakes. My loving husband, Jeff who has been my rock, my trusted friend to hold my hand and help guide me. A lot has been put onto his shoulders too. I have purposely left much of the other family members out of the book for their privacy, because it has only been my perspective, a mother's point of view and how I see my life's journey. It is therefore very detailed about our sons and their travel through life. This does not mean that my husband, Jeff, and our other children, Sarah and Amanda are not important, because they are and certainly, they are by no means least. A lot of time was focused on the boys as they were growing. They needed it. But I see this has worked for all of us because I see you all as caring, loving, understanding, and forgiving people.

I also want to dedicate this book to Desiree. It was Desiree who made me promise to write the book because of the interesting tales I would tell her about our lads when we had a cuppa. Desiree was not one to let go and asked me (several times) had I finished yet. It has taken many years of fun and laughter, anguish and joy to put these words on paper.

Last but by no means least, I want to thank the carers, the support workers of our lads. With the help of NDIS, they have been an intricate part of the process of the lads learning new skills, maintaining old ones, and encouraging the lads' independence. They keep us updated and they have the very best intentions for the lads in mind. This allows us to relax and chase our own aspirations, dreams and desires.

Maryborough has been a good town for the family and particularly for our lads. It is small enough that most people know them and are caring of them. They seem to watch out for them. There are some very kind people out there. Maryborough is large enough to provide all necessary essentials for an independent life. And for me, it allows me to have spies everywhere! I have learnt it really does take a village to raise a child!

Introduction

When our child was born, we grieved like we had lost our boy. You see he was born with Down's Syndrome. He has an intellectual disability. Down's Syndrome, (also known as trisomy 21), is a chromosomal condition where there is an extra copy of genetic material on the 21st chromosome. At the time he was born in 1976, people were commonly called mongoloid because of the features that are usually present in a person who has Downs Syndrome. The incidence is increased with older or very young parents. At 24 years old I did not fit into any of the categories of increased risk to give birth to a child who has Downs Syndrome. Back then babies were commonly institutionalized or locked away so no one would see them or stare at them. There were minimal opportunities for them to be independent and engage in the community. Thankfully times have changed.

Even though we thought it at the time, I want other parents to know that it is not the end of the world, it is indeed a very new and interesting beginning. Our lads have taught me so much! The intent of this book is to show that even the most negative events can be seen in a positive way. I guess it is about putting yourself in the shoes of your child with the disability and looking at the world through their eyes. *You know it is beautiful behind those eyes.* My lads see the positive in everyone. Now that's a real talent! They both have a wicked sense of humour and are very loving as I will endeavour to show. There is always two ways of looking at things and sometimes it is difficult to understand someone who has limited understanding, who doesn't tick all the boxes. Take the time to find out; take the time it takes. This means we take the knocks too. Although some people seem to be bias or don't understand, I have to say that the world has changed and is changing and people don't stare in shock as they used to 46 years ago when our son, Jason was born. There is quite a difference in social attitude now. We enjoyed our parenthood and so we adopted another son, Mark who was born 34 years ago also with Down's Syndrome. Yes, we have 2 sons who have Downs Syndrome as we dearly wanted another child. We understood, and probably not quite prepared for, their vulnerabilities, the excitement and love they bought us, and the road less travelled we had by having 2 children with Down's Syndrome. We have enjoyed the challenges, and the fun they have bought into our lives. Jason is 12 years older. We were soon to realise they are chalk and cheese, and very individual! They have both given us many challenges and indeed many delights, some of which, if my memory serves me well, I will detail in this book. These events may not be in chronological order as they are according to and relying on my memory. One thing I do know we are never bored. We certainly know we are living!

I do know that my husband and I have to be sure of our value base in order to survive. Yes, I know that this needs to be secure for any child. I have found it needs to be very secure for both of you as the trials, the boundaries, the successes, that a child with an intellectual disability provides, and are very different and complex. There needs to be defined unity. Although a child may have limited understanding don't ever make the mistake that they don't understand. Our boys have a very uncanny way of seeing through people, the good in people, and the holes in parents!!!

But this book is about my perceptions, and my perspective as a mother and how my life had changed because of Jason's birth and the impacts it had on us as a family. It was through Jason's birth that changed my whole pathway in life and my dedications. It changed us so much that while parenting Jason, we wanted to adopt another child with Down's Syndrome. My whole career path changed. For goodness' sake I was just a check out chick for Woolworths. I had no idea what job satisfaction was, until I worked in disabilities. Since then, I have worked in the mental health sector, all of which I would not have thought about except for my life's journey. All our children have taught me to love, advocate, nurture and protect. We made many mistakes along the way too. We were allowed to make mistakes, there is no parent manual.

Jeff and I had to be sure of what we viewed as important in life, what is right and what is wrong and be prepared to be flexible, particularly as the child becomes an adult. I don't want to have the eternal child; we wanted our lads to be the most independent they can possibly be. This is where the grey areas come in, it was certainly difficult not to wrap them up in cotton wool and certainly Mark has crossed every boundary given to him, because he can! That's our Mark! It all has paid off though. It doesn't mean I haven't been sneaky because I certainly have and I guess as he reads this, he will know all my secrets!! While we tried to impart a positive lifestyle and value system for all our children, sometimes they have to trial it and go against our wishes, just to prove it all for themselves. It is part of developing and becoming your own person with your own set of values – and hello - they could be different to yours! This requires experimentation and natural consequences. The best we could do was to prepare them the best we could and be there. As I said I also was very creative in making sure the cards stacked up for them. The values that I feel are really important, the lads may not. For example, trying to   instil manners in children, not only does it mean they need to know when and how to use them, they have got to want to use them which means understanding people's expectations and their feelings. If these senses are foreign to a person or there is an opposing attitude, then it can be very difficult. I found it important to try and work with them with plenty of acceptance, approval, and praise - not against them – oh did I forget to say they can be stubborn! However, this can be a positive trait and a good survival technique. Perhaps we should call it -- determination. We found it important to praise even the smallest successes and steps that others may take for granted. It was important for me not to differentiate my lads from the other two children. So, they had chores just like the rest of the household. They may not have been able to do as much or indeed, as well, but they did them anyway. If the bed wasn't made very well, it was okay. I felt it was important not to make it after them but praise their efforts and give them a sense of responsibility and belonging. Let them own it!

All the good intentions and values under the sun will be tried and tested and if you pass the tests, you'll enjoy the moments. I took the time to enjoy the moments and I can say that if I had my time again, I would do things differently as I know so much more and also how to be assertive. I have made many mistakes some of which I will divulge, some you will be the judge, and others –well now - that would be telling!

I think that the time you invest into your children is never wasted but we had four children and I didn't want the time spent teaching the boys to be undervalued or opposed by others, particularly I didn't want the 2 girls to feel neglected or jealous of the extra time spent with the boys. I'm not sure I counteracted that entirely but as a family, when they were young, we managed and now as a family unit we are stronger. I do believe because of the interaction of all the family, particularly their siblings, because of their high involvement in the community, the boys are very high functioning and very independent today. They can and do contribute and engage in the community in many ways which I will detail some of the ways in this book.

Remember I said they were chalk and cheese. They are both very high functioning. Jason is unassuming, funny and had a job for approximately 25 years in a Piggery, he owns his own home, loves his bowling and was a black belt in Karate. He has now married Julie. Mark is a people's person, great conversationalist, loves writing (and I'm sure he will be writing his own book and contributing to this one). He is thoughtful and considerate, and has tested every boundary, guideline and limit thrown to him! He functions by testing everything, getting himself into all sorts of strife and I think you'll agree by the time you finish this book; it does make for interesting reading and an interesting life! Life has never been dull!

CHAPTER ONE

How the family started

In 1976 we had already one child, Sarah who was 16 months old. I was eight months pregnant when I received some horrible news; news that nobody should have to receive. My brother, Russell who was 21 years of age was killed in a motor bike accident. This was out of the blue. It just wasn't fair. He only just started putting his life together when the accident had occurred. The grief I felt was intolerable and excruciating and the baby I was carrying was threatening to come a month early because of this.

I was still mourning when finally, our son was born, one month later, with the cord wrapped around his neck 3 times. I remember that when he was born, I looked at him and felt he'd been here before. He seemed like an old man and I'm still not sure why I thought this, perhaps the poor muscle toning. I remember my husband saying what a huge tongue he had --- and he has --- it protruded a lot. I remember thinking that the doctor who delivered him was not happy or smiling. I thought congratulations should have been in order or some nice words like 'you have a beautiful baby boy'. I thought this was strange. He was whisked away from us and they said it was to clean him up, but they were taking so long. The more I asked the more I wasn't told. Remember this was 1976. They just said they had to check him out. Hours later my elation was starting to wane, and I could feel that there may be something they weren't telling us. I kept asking questions and anxiety was welling within both of us. I just knew something was not right. Jeff seemed to have worked out in his head that it was reasonable and that they were just checking everything out. Finally, the doctor told us that he suspected our child had Downs Syndrome or he said we might know it better as Mongoloid. He would know definitely as soon as the tests came back. I looked in disbelief and then I cried. I cried for the loss of my brother, I cried for nature being so cruel, I cried for all the unsaid plans and expectations we had for our baby. I cried saying to Jeff "not your boy; not your boy" as I knew it was important to him to have a boy. I just cried and cried; we both did.

We received the test results and he is indeed Downs Syndrome. We received some advice from the doctor. That was to give him up and put him in an institution. Back then this was the normal thing to do. The doctor said, "he probably won't read or write and it will be better to get on with your own lives". My mum and dad felt the same, that we wouldn't manage. I thought that Downs Syndrome was someone who would never walk, never feed himself or communicate in any way, so I started to feel the same way. I asked for a tablet to stop my milk while we sorted this mess out. Remember except when I first delivered my son, I still hadn't seen him, more than 24 hours later. My husband was equally determined that we should keep him – God bless him!

A nurse came in at that time and asked if we knew what Downs Syndrome was. We confessed that we really had no knowledge of the condition. She proceeded to explain. That he might look a little different because his eyes may be an almond shape and slanted upwards, that he has an extra-large tongue which might impede his language clarity and his language may be intellectually minimized, he may be shorter in stature with shorter limbs but he will talk, he will walk, and he will learn. She continued that they are usually the most loving, gentlest people on earth. I blubbered "Bring him to me". I am forever grateful to that nurse.

When he was bought to us, we just cuddled and cuddled him. She left us alone and came back later. She explained and showed us that he had a single crease instead of a double crease across both palms, he would have poor muscle toning and a larger than normal space between the big and second toes. People with Down's are usually short in stature. He could have some extra health concerns such as a higher risk for congenital heart defects, chest and ear infections, thyroid dysfunction and obesity and dementia. Often, they do not live to old age. She did say that medicine was improving with more healthy outcomes likely.

Lucky I never did take the tablet to dry up my milk so I started to feed him. I was warned that he may not be able to suckle as well because of his huge tongue. We managed in hospital although it became difficult later.

I had had him two days now and still in hospital when we were told of a conference about Downs Syndrome and a professor was speaking. I cannot remember anything about it as I was blubbering quietly down the back of the room the whole time, but I do remember one thing that gave me courage. I remember the professor saying, "and why can't a person with Downs Syndrome become a bus driver". I went back to hospital knowing that it was up to us and he would be given every opportunity to be the very best he can be – by hook or by crook. I was prepared to move mountains and at last I felt a glimmer of courage. Jeff said he was ours and that we need to do the best we can.

We went to my parent's home with our brand-new baby; we called him Jason, just to stay a couple of days. I remember people and friends visiting and not knowing what to say. Giving us "Oh I'm so sorry for you", Hey we had a beautiful baby, look at him, don't apologize, this is a blessing. It annoyed me but it was a difficult time for everyone and people aren't sure how to act.

For us, it was the not knowing what the future holds for a person with Downs Syndrome. We were sailing blind. Unconsciously I think you have the whole life mapped out of all the things they might get up to and I felt Jason might not be given the chance. Time would tell though. I'm sure mum thought I was off with the fairies without a good grasp of what was ahead and I remember panic hitting me as I stepped through the door for the first time of leaving hospital. How are we going to cope, we live in a caravan out in the bush, traveling in the forestry, wherever Jeff's work took him. What were our needs going to be now? I decided to take it a step at a time so we nestled in to our caravan about 30 kms away from Gympie in a very pretty spot in the forestry. Our caravan was big and the kids had double bunks in the back along with shower and toilet. There was plenty of room and we soon settled in and got into a routine.

He was an easy-going baby and just a joy to be around. He certainly showed his personality. I began to find he wasn't suckling very well and I would express my milk and feed him by bottle because I thought that might be easier for him. I was determined to feed him my milk as long as I could because it is a natural defence against colds and chest infections. He seemed to be blue in the mornings when I went to pick him up. This was worrying and I needed to see a doctor. We went to a paediatrician who said that he had a hole in his heart. He felt it would be detrimental to have an operation as it was a huge step to take (and in those days, it was even bigger). We were to wait and see. Now I know that this little fella was really not well as he couldn't suckle now at all and I was feeding him by teaspoon, eye dropper, any method that worked. One feed would run into another. Sarah would be on the bed with me playing while I tried to feed him. I tried to involve her as much as possible. I felt so bad that I couldn't give her some special time just for her. She was only 17 months but a lovely temperament and took everything in her stride. This type of feeding went on for months but I noticed that it did start to improve and again I tried him with a bottle and he was suckling. I tried my breast again and he took it. When we went back to the paediatrician the hole in Jason's heart had closed. This, he said was most unusual. I don't know if you believe in the power of prayer but I swear it was Jeff's mum's prayers that helped him! I then could feed him by breast until he was 15 months old.

He never did get a cold until I weaned him!

I visited a community nurse in Gympie once a week who would weigh him and offer support, knowledge and encouragement. He went through all his milestones on time, and she explained that this would change as he got older, the gap would increase. She was right. He walked at 2 years and 3 months. He was carried on my hip everywhere I went. He was getting heavy, and I was weary. Besides my husband (who was at work all day and could talk to work mates), the nurse was the only other person I would see week in and week out, once a week. Jeff is fine with his own company, and he didn't really mind, in fact he enjoyed the solitude, but I was becoming isolated and lonely especially as we were moving around a lot in the van to follow Jeff's work. I was so busy offering lots of sensory stimulation for the children, I didn't really notice what was happening to me -- back then. Also, there was no babysitting services for me to tap into, so I had the children constantly, which is fine but just now and then it would have been good to have a reprieve, like going to appointments, shopping, everything, Jason was constantly on my hip while I carried him, and Sarah walked along side me. Relatives were too far away and I don't think they felt like they could manage the children with Jason's special needs. In fact, there was never any reprieve as they grew older to be able to have just a little time out.

We decided to buy a block of land near the area where Jeff was going to be working most of the time - that is near Maryborough, Qld. I love Maryborough for its people and for its country atmosphere. We found 6.25 acres in the country town of Tiaro and decided to buy this. We didn't have any money so we relied heavily on the family to support us with the deposit (and I think it was about $2000 which was a lot back then) and we would pay them back. I wanted to have electricity so I could keep Jason cool in summer and warm in winter instead of the generator which went only at night. I was still concerned about his heart.

Jeff built a shed and we divided the rooms with wardrobes and we had a wood stove. We also could have some pets for the kids, and the kids bottle fed a lamb which I might add, became a nuisance as he was the biggest ram I have ever seen. He would jump on the beds as soon as the door was opened in our shed. He lined up with the neighbour's dairy cows for a feed. They were frightened of him too. He'd get through our fencing. He eventually had to go as we were worried; he might hurt the children as he was starting to butt people. We had chooks too and Jason was very fascinated by them. We were quite snuggled in there and as the kids grew so did my growing desire to have another child. After all he was just a fluke according to our blood tests, it shouldn't happen again.

We paid off the block to our parents and we decided to move again. This time we moved just over the hill. We used this former block as a deposit for these 132 acres and asked if the owner could throw in an old, dilapidated house that had been used as a shed for farm machinery for a long time. The house was actually two houses pulled together by bullock dray and was over a hundred years old. I could see what she (the house) was meant to look like, and the owner agreed to throw it in the deal. We would have to pay to shift it which was just across the railway line and about 1kilometre from where it had been resting.

As the kids grew, we worked hard to complete the house. We cleaned and painted it inside and out, with all its grease and dirt. We had help from family to clean it. Jeff put new verandahs and roof on it and pulled down the back of it where the white ants had only just started their journey through our home before it was shifted. He rebuilt most of this and I remember while he was building a bathroom which was now going to be built on the verandah. We were about 200 metres from the highway, and we could look out at the highway while taking a bath with the tarpaulins flapping - I thought we might have had a pile up of cars on the highway!!! That was finished by winter as we were freezing. I became a carpenter too and built-in cupboards, walls and benches.

By this time Jason was becoming a wild boy when our second daughter Amanda was born. Mandy was an easy-going child who was happy all the time. She was threatened to be delivered too early, 7 months gestation, so I had to be very quiet and not lift or do anything until her time had come to be born which happened at full term. It had been very difficult though to have bed rest with Jason being very active.

Now Jason was becoming a bit of an escape artist and it wasn't long when I had locked the veranda that he found innovative ways of scaling it and running. I think it only stopped me from getting to him as quickly!

Jason loved the chooks too and would always be down at the chook pen. He loved to teach them how to swim and would often have them in the cow trough catching them and playing with them, laughing his head off. And I'm sure they could have swum if he had only given them the chance!!

He definitely needed supervision. He just had more energy than me and I would sit down to rest just a minute when it was just too quiet.

Oh no – so by the time I had checked the chook pen and his usual spots he had escaped well and truly. Jason would run so fast. We also had a lot of land and at the time we couldn't afford cattle, so the grass was as tall as Jason and he was not able to be seen; not that he wanted to be found! We weren't sure where to look if he wasn't in the chook pen. We bought a dog when Amanda was born. This dog was half German Shepherd and half Collie. This dog was very protective of all the children and most photos taken back in those days Shep was seen in the background with tongue hanging out or slurping on the cheek of a child. He was a beautiful, very intelligent dog and he loved the kids and they loved him. He was very protective. I never taught him, but somehow, he just knew when I asked him "where's Jason". Shep would take off and go to where Jason was (even though we couldn't find him!). He would bark and bark until I could get there and when Jason was still determined to run off that dog would stand in front of Jay. One day when Jason was particularly determined, Shep put his mouth around Jason's wrist. I thought oh, no! but when I finally got to Jason there wasn't a mark on him.

I had many miscarriages in the next few years, so we decided to adopt a baby who had Down's Syndrome. When Amanda was seven years old the adoption processes were completed and Mark came into our lives. He was a beautiful little baby, 5 weeks old with no problems feeding and sleeping.

When he was just a baby, I put him out in the front yard under our trees in his pram. I went inside for a moment and I'd come back out and our dog, Shep, would be there guarding him, and that dog would not move.

When the kids were on the trampoline the dog was always with them and he would be underneath the trampoline barking as the kids were jumping. This was annoying for me, but the kids loved it. If he was allowed, I'm sure the dog would have been jumping on the trampoline with them! That dog was the best friend the kids could ever have.

For the kids we eventually afforded some sheep, but the local dogs had killed a few through the night time, just for the sake of killing, not eating; leaving the sheep to die a slow, horrible death. We then decided to bring the sheep up to the yards near the house at night. We went on foot with Shep's help of course to round them up. At night Shep was always locked on our verandah. The verandah went right around the house. We soon learnt that Shep had special ways of barking. By the way he barked he would tell us if there was a stray dog on the property, or another bark if it was a ewe lambing.

And I knew that when the kids were with Shep they were pretty safe. He would kill snakes if they were near us and I would only have to mention "Shep, snake" even if he was on the verandah away from us and he would leap from the top step of the back verandah missing all the other seven steps and come to our aid.

Unfortunately, our beautiful Shep was afraid of storms and would hide when they were around. He didn't come inside the house, so he found somewhere in different places outside. One day when there was a storm brewing, I had to go out in the car. As I reversed our 4x4 car out of the carport I heard a yelp. Just one but one I'll never forget. Shep was 9 years old. I had run over him. I put him in the car and took him straight to the vet, a half hour away. The vet said that his heart was on the wrong side of his chest and organs had been damaged. It cost us a fortune, but he survived. It took him time to recover but recover he did. About 1 year later he was on the verandah with us when a whip snake was also on the verandah. I didn't see it in time or I would have asked Shep to leave it as now he was a little sluggish and his heart was obviously under strain. The snake although not particularly poisonous bit Shep. Our children were around there too. Our beautiful Shep took his last breath within minutes. Our family were so upset, particularly Amanda, as Shep was born the same time as Amanda 10 years earlier and she had never known life without him, and I was very upset knowing that I contributed to his demise.

Techniques

I spent all my time trying to encourage the boys to do and play like the others and I would add many sensory stimulation and educational exercises for them all. I did home educational sessions with Sarah to spend more quality time with her before she started school. It paid off. Both the boys have learnt and have always strived to reach their full potential, they both have a good sense of humour. The girls were very good at helping them too.

Jason has a large tongue, Mark does not. Jason's tongue would always protrude so we used to tap a finger on our mouths a couple of times, and he knew that meant he had to put his tongue inside his mouth. It wasn't just that there wasn't much room inside his mouth, it was poor muscle toning as well. It was a great signal for us to do without saying anything in front of people, I would just tap my mouth twice and he would instantly put his tongue in. This I would do a hundred times a day. Now that he is an adult this is not needed. He keeps it inside his mouth all the time.

Mark's tongue is tongue-tied but they said that they wouldn't do anything. Probably it's not bad enough. I have to say it has never stopped his speech or his language. Boy, can that lad talk!! It wasn't always so and while the lads were trying to put language and sentences together, we used methods to ensure they could get their message across. You can imagine how frustrating it must be to want to say something or your needs met and no one can understand. For Jason he used gestures and I would always insist that he would try and say the word too, even though it was very unclear. I understood him all the time, but others couldn't, so years later with Mark, we decided to use Makaton sign language which is a universal sign language. It offers symbols and it is much easier to learn for someone with limited dexterity. He became very proficient at it very quickly. This way, teachers and others could understand him. His pre-school teacher was very good at involving the whole class and Mark soon became the teacher! The whole class did a song, singing it and using Makaton as well. It was lovely to see how involved he was, just because this teacher normalised the fact that Mark had difficulties with speech. I was concerned though that he would use Makaton instead of spoken language, but I always insisted that he try speaking as well. He soon used spoken language and if people couldn't understand, it was only then he would use Makaton. Mark would try out many big words to see where they fitted and it was definitely hard not to laugh sometimes as he would say words like "don't be dicklous" [ridiculous] and we would have to decipher what he was saying because he would put them in the wrong context. Confiscate was one word that took me a long time to understand. But try he did, and he still does. They both have very good speech and language and use complex sentences and you can understand them. I think though the clarity is just a little different but understandable. And you know what -- they both read and write – very well!!! But at this point I have to say that the whole family was involved in assisting the boys to develop good communication skills. I remember one day we were going past the Kentucky fried chicken place. Jason was about seven years old and communicating very well but at times would be stumped to say what he wanted to say. He really wanted to stop at Kentucky fried chicken and started saying "yucky, yucky, yucky". Miss three-year-old, Amanda said "Say after me Jason, Chu-ck, Chucky fried chicken". She was pretty cute. Out of the mouths of babes!

    I never realised what characters our boys could be and what innovative decision making and channels of thoughts these guys could have that would keep me in a constant state of amazement and laughter and love. I am still constantly surprised and amazed and I think you'll see why.

CHAPTER TWO

The School Years

When Jason went to school there was no opportunity to send him to, a so-called, normal school. We were told that this is because "he wouldn't get the expertise he required to learn like at the Special School and in a so-called normal school, it could turn out the focus of attention could be Jason against the whole class," – a teacher told me. I went along with this because I figured that it could be difficult and I didn't want him to miss out either. Jason started at the special school at 6 years old.

Jason loved school and I was a constant parent there. He learnt by the rules very quickly and was never much trouble. He learnt to his capacity and loved to do manual arts and all sorts of activities using his hands however it was starting to become difficult to keep him motivated.

Jason always found difficulty in chewing different textured foods when he was younger. He didn't like any foods where there was chewing involved, so he'd pick foods that were soft – like ice cream (don't all kids?) and bread – and not much else except for vitamin tablets. I think this limited diet was because of his large tongue and poor muscle toning when chewing his food. Using a vibrator, I used to massage his tongue and round his mouth to help with muscle control. I knew it was important to encourage him to eat all sorts of food and have a balanced diet. I soon found he'd eat anything as long as it had tomato sauce on it! I drew the line at his wheat bix though! By the time he went to school, Jason's diet had improved and he would eat almost anything.

Jason had difficulty with spelling and although we'd spend many an hour going through his homework, he never did grasp it and couldn't get the concept of verbs. He wrote well (without some of the correct spelling) and he read okay, there was difficulty in some large words, but he could read and you should know that I was determined on that score. He had difficulty also with math, but he had enough knowledge to count money and know how much items were and how much change he should get. And when he had his own pocket money, he certainly was making sure I got it right! It takes a lot of practice though and when he went to a shop or bank, I'd be standing back behind him, and making the queue wait, while he slowly counted it out with precise determination. Most people had a smile on their face because Jason talks loudly, and he was so pleased with himself. I'm sure the rest of the shop could hear his joy and his laughter. It tickled most people. Jason has a very wicked laugh and sense of humour; it is quite infectious. It comes straight from the heart. He quickly learnt the value of everyday money use, but the bigger picture money was very foreign to him and still is.

The school was very patient with him and would have him involved in every stage of manual arts. He had a little difficulty with bringing his index finger and thumb together in a coordinated movement. He really liked manual arts though - especially when he presented his achievement to me for my birthday or Mother's Day, I'm not sure which it was. In fact, I wrote a speech for Toastmasters about one such present which I will include here. It's these little gifts, these little achievements that are celebrated so much with our family because it is done with so much determination, painstakingly and with the greatest of love.

Those positive Ions

One present I received for Christmas was a beautiful chair. It was a little different because it was very small, and this chair was made out of paddle pop sticks. It had a concertina effect and opened out into this long bench seat. It had about one hundred very small nails in it which had been cut off at the back, with the exception of a few that were missed. I know that because my fingers found them, ouch! And I thought about all the months it had taken for this young lad with an intellectual disability to make it, and all the care and concentration it would have taken for him to finish it. How he would have anguished over the small parts his hands couldn't master.

My eyes were close to tears as I saw the glee and anticipation on my son's face when he presented his gift to me.

And I thought about the courage and determination it took for him to finish this gift. The same determination that it took for him to ride his bike. Oh, how he tried! He had scratches and bruises all over him as he fell over and over -- and over again. But he'd keep trying --until finally he did it.

I remember when he played cricket with others and how they taunted him because he couldn't play properly. But he still stayed and then I noticed how little by little they changed. They showed him little things and then showed him again. I could see there was a new found respect for this person they called "retard". They looked past the exterior and into his beautiful soul.

When Jason was born, we thought what a tragedy to have a child with an intellectual disability.

Oh, how we grieved. We grieved for those lost plans we had for our child; we grieved for what he wasn't going to get out of life; we grieved for the person he couldn't be.

But within our sorrow something stirred within us. Through this sorrow we also felt love; Love so strong that no man could destroy. We felt the acceptance of who he was and the joys as he achieved even the smallest success. Oh, how we celebrated these!

We asked why this should happen to us.

I think I know why.

Through this child we love so much - came a greater understanding in life. Through his eyes we started to see the world differently.

Do you know it's beautiful from behind those eyes of his?

Through his eyes there's a happy knack of finding the gems in people.

I notice that I can see more clearly through the barriers of people around me, I can see their honesty, their integrity, their genuine spirit, the gems of who they really are. And from behind those barriers, I see a person who may be branded a reject, but I see the basics of living and giving come so easily for him.

It may be raining outside but inside it is perfectly fine.

I have learnt that when the chips are down and -- especially when the chips are down --- it is then that you search for those gems in life, what is important and what is not. I have also learnt that life is too short to worry about what is not or never will be.

If I hadn't suffered miscarriages, I would not have met a lady named Rose in the hospital who also taught me valuable lessons on life. You see she was dying of leukemia. She was so beautiful inside that we became really good friends until she died.

This lady with all the pain she suffered still saw the little gems in everyone. She had everyone smitten by her natural beauty and charm she possessed from within.

She took great pleasure in everything and cared about everyone. And she saw the positives in everyone. She only *ever* cared to comment on the positives of people.

She seemed to be like a magnet and drew people to her – with positive ions you might say, she was so nice to be near.

Of course, the trick is to find the gems. It's easy to see what is wrong, but by focusing on the positive ions - now that's when you locate your gems. Look into the hearts and *you'll* find them.

Although many years have passed, I often smile as I pass that treasured chair that stands pride of place on our mantelpiece. And I look at that beautiful paddle pop chair and think of our tragedy that turned out to be our gem.

The gems of life ---The roses of time. How we've been blessed.

So, remember keep looking! There *are* positive ions near you!
End of Speech.

School taught Jason many skills of basic living as well as planning and structure. There was one aspect that was bothersome to me though and that was hygiene. Jason didn't have the dexterity to wash his hands well and to be careful in the toilets as far as germs go. He also had to be reminded about washing his hands which of course the school could not always do. He didn't see the point. It was difficult to nag when I wasn't there and because there were a number of people who had infectious health concerns at school, I was concerned. But Jason gained friendships there, and this was great as he hadn't been able to make friends before, except for our friends (that is family friends). They were his friends and he didn't seem to go out of his way to make new ones. School taught him the value of team work. Jason didn't go to high school, he stayed at the special school until he turned 18 yrs.

Jason wanted friendships from school and if this was to be so then I would have to partner him. That is, it took a third person to develop and maintain the friendships. You know if you ask another person who has an intellectual disability or/and behavioural difficulties to your place, chances are that their parents have to also be involved. Some parents are so worn out that it is just too much effort to invite your son over or visa - versa.

Because people with disabilities come with their own personal encumbrance it is difficult for burnt out parents to want to spend the time and effort in planning a social outing. There are difficulties when they become teenagers – you know hormones on legs! I think people don't realize how important friendships are particularly for people who have disabilities. It often has to be nurtured by someone else other than the friends involved. When Jason forms friendships with people without disabilities I sometimes need to monitor it for a while because unfortunately there are unscrupulous people out there as I will explain later.

Jason had made some very good local friendships. They lived just down the road. They included Jason in many activities and as always, they all had a great time. They are still friends today. He loved to go fishing, swimming, bike riding and camping down by our creek with these boys. Our next-door neighbours played well with him but when they adopted a young lad, Matthew, he and Jason got on very well. They had lots of fun and Jason was feeling included because he had friends. He got on well with most people at school, but he never did really have kids from school come to visit home even when we tried. As I stated earlier, they often had many disabilities and it was difficult for parents to allow it, especially when we live so far out of town (26 kms). In that way they miss out and so does Jason. He didn't have people stay overnight.

School for Mark was a different story however as the times had changed (some 12 years later) and we really wanted him to be part of the community and integrate into a normal school life. We decided to enrol him into the local Tiaro Preschool to see how he went. He had a fantastic teacher, David who included Mark every small step of the way. Mark grew confident and he certainly did the best he could. I can remember well, their concert they did at the end of the year. Mark shone as he acted his part, and I might be a little prejudice here, but he was so cute! And when they came to singing, they sung it and did Makaton signing too. Mark was so important and the teacher made him so included – I could feel the tears well in my eyes. Because of this inclusiveness and the skill of the teacher, Mark had many friends who would play with him, and some would mother him – either way he was an important part of the team.

However, at the end of the year, we were advised by the "experts" to keep Mark in preschool to give him the very best chance of succeeding. I had reservations and expressed them because he had friendships he wanted to maintain, and I knew he would be looked after by them. His friends just loved him and he loved them! I didn't succeed and the picture became very different for the following year. He now wouldn't be able to play with his mates either as they were in a different part of the school and it was frowned upon. This was the worst decision of our lives.

He had a new pre-school teacher and a new group. The teacher's expertise with integration was not as accomplished as her predecessor and Mark soon became ostracized and lonely. He was often trying to play with his mates from the first year of preschool, but the school wanted to avoid this. I remember having a conversation with this new preschool teacher who said "that when they are all singing, they all look at Mark because he doesn't say the words, he just says "blahhh, blahhh, blahhh" all the way through, and the kids wonder what on earth is wrong with him. He just doesn't fit in". She said that Mark would have to adapt – not the rest of the class. The only hope I held was that things would be different next year because I couldn't seem to make a difference in this scenario. I wasn't as assertive back then – quite mousy actually. That was going to change! Having a child with disabilities certainly hones those skills! I felt that things would have been much better if she had coped better and included Mark more and his attempts at language. He soon didn't want to stay at preschool, but we felt that a new teacher in Grade one might help.

The following year proved to be worse with the same children just being mean and horrid and although the new teacher tried, and expressed her concerns, there was nothing that she tried changed the situation. Being a small school if your classmates were against you, there wasn't much else for you. We left him in that school because he may have the same horrors elsewhere and I wanted him to try and work past it. The world was not going to be a bed of roses for him. Mark did well all the same in class and although he didn't keep up, he was learning lots. He was now starting to read and write – and you know how I feel about the lads being able to read and write! He couldn't grasp adding up, he just couldn't remember and had to do this on his fingers, but he is very accomplished and a wiz with a calculator. If he had a calculator in his hand, he could work out any sum—and complicated ones too. When Mark was still in grade 2 a horrific thing happened. The classroom buddies decided to play a trick on him. So, they all peed into a soft drink can and told him they had a drink for him! He took one drink and then spat it out. Now my assertive skills were about to be developed. I was horrified, upset, frightened (for his health) and the bristles went up on the back of my neck as I marched up to the school. The teachers were doing everything they possibly could, I know, but it didn't stop me from saying what I thought and how upset I was and what were they going to do to prevent this hostile environment my lad found himself in. I have to say Lyn (his teacher) was just as upset and dismayed. They gave educational chats to the whole class, reprimanded the involved lads and gave them consequences. Everything did seem to be a little better for Mark after this, although he was starting to play up in school. This may have been to cover the fact that he wasn't keeping up with his work or the fact that trying your hardest all the time is difficult and to have a reprieve on something that you are good at, gives self-esteem and courage to keep trying. Mark was starting to give up. He fell further behind as the tasks required of him were more complicated. He was learning and now he read well and his writing was so neat. He wrote all the time he just loved it. He wrote down words of songs, poetry, everything he could put his hands on –and you know how I felt about his reading and writing!!

He went through his grades fine as he still had the same teacher, and she really did whatever she could to include Mark and have a good teaching environment. When he went on to grade four though he had a different teacher. From the moment he was in this grade, I heard everything Mark wasn't able to do. He wrote in his report card –there was nothing positive there. Now I am usually very patient and have good understanding of people's different natures, but this teacher was starting to annoy me. Now you know about my assertive skills they had been honed up already and he was about to find out how much! I told the teacher that I knew exactly what Mark was unable to do and I didn't expect him to keep up. I didn't want it to be him against the rest of the class, but he was funded a teacher's aide to assist Mark, use them! I really only needed to hear the positive stuff of what Mark was able to do because frankly he doesn't need to be knocked down any more than he was already, and he and I needed some positives. Every report card I received from that point on was terrific. It didn't have to be unrealistic just fair for Mark's abilities –and it was. He had two years with that teacher and then he had Gary for the next two. Now I have to say while I didn't agree with Gary all the time, he kept me in the loop what was and what wasn't happening. He told me the pit falls and the strengths of Mark and this was good. I must say here it wasn't that I didn't want to hear the negatives I just didn't want to hear only negative stuff. I knew where Mark was exactly. Gary was easy going and while some say a bit too easy going it certainly helped Mark to thrive. He learnt the recorder in those years and although he couldn't read music, Mark certainly played it well - by ear! He loves music and he loves singing although his singing isn't melodious! He knows every song and singer I think that ever was. When he left that school, I remember the great review he received on his report card where Gary wished him well for the future. He stated he would do well because "He's the man!" Mark had become sure of himself and felt he could do anything he set his mind to. I had so many reservations at that time, and I wondered what challenges high school would bring. Believe me we encountered many!

Mark loves routine and although I'm not the most routine person, he knew what and when things were to happen at home. His first day at high school was not routine and I soon realized it never would be. Although high school tried the routine and the roster thing, they had their own problems, and it wasn't working.

It was chaos from the very first day. Mark was supposed to be in one room on the roster and then he would be redirected to another. After confusion he would start to be in trouble for being late. When he wanted to finish his work, they would say that he had to start something else. Now I'm saying this from Mark's point of view now, because I'm sure the school didn't see it this way. It was one of many arguments I had with the school. Mark became a little despondent with the school teachers and determination or should I say stubbornness became his forefront. This unruly roster was very confusing for many months and eventually Mark started bucking the system and the teachers. He would just plonk himself down on the verandah and refuse to move. Can you imagine how humiliating it would be for a top science teacher with Batchelor degrees and lots of experience and expertise with the chemical compounds and molecular changes trying to talk to -- and prise this young man from the verandah floor with a stubbornness that is incomparable? It wasn't working!

His schooling was difficult and as he was becoming a young man, he also felt that he could oppose most requests and what the teachers wanted. He was also given the opportunity to do work experience. He was very excited. It required me to get him there and to keep close contact with the place he was to have his experience. I spent a lot of time explaining how important it was for his work life and if he did really well, then they would know him and if they had vacancies later on, he might get a job. He was all for it, he tried his very best and we made sure he was always on time. I would take him to the place where he was to work and drop him off 5 – 8 mins before he started work. It was probably the only time I didn't have to nag him to get ready as I did for him to go to school. He just loved his work experience and his newfound independence and responsibility. He tried so hard to do it right and they loved him. He finally felt he was able to do something right. He was becoming quite rebellious at school, so the teachers took from him swimming, tennis and computer as a punishment. They said they were running out of things to take from him. When I spoke to them, I said that they were the only things that he was good at and really enjoyed. I asked that they use these instead as rewards for when he did what he was to do. This did not happen; he was being punished for any little thing they could find and wait for it – they took away his work experience!!! Now you know that assertive skill I had just proclaimed; it was time to use it. The teacher even said that he would get there half an hour early to his work experience and this was a great inconvenience to the workplace. This was not the case as I always took him and watched him walk inside and I emphasized this. I spoke to the hierarchy of the education system trying to keep him going to work experience, but there was no resolve. I went to the director of education, but it seemed to be a closed book as the teachers stuck together except for one. They made me feel like I was lowly and dramatic and my complaints, I feel, were not taken seriously. Still, he couldn't go back to work experience and then he lost the whole term not being able to participate in work experience. He lost interest after that and just didn't want to bother any more. I didn't know what to do.

Anyway, if the desired effect was for him to become even more rebellious and not care about anything, school, work, anything then they achieved it!! He had absolutely nothing to look forward to and I am so displeased with the way the whole thing was handled. These teachers were in the special unit of the high school. They should be equipped with skills for disabilities to bring out the best in people. As I mentioned there was one teacher who was an ally and who believed things could have been handled differently for Mark. She also seemed to be the only one who could get desired outcomes from him. She always kept me in the loop and was really good to talk to. She now was at logger heads with other teaching staff herself and ended up leaving her employment. I think it is important to know that you have rights too and while Mark was classified as needing high needs as far as teacher's aides went; he still shared that resource with others, and I didn't feel he got what he needed, and I certainly think they devalued anything a mere parent might have to say. A parent, I might add, who knows him best, who knows how to get the best out of him. Anyway, school wasn't working for him but what else was there. Where he had worked for work experience, they thought he was unreliable because one day he just didn't turn up. The teacher didn't have the courtesy to talk to the workplace and say that he was unable to finish his work until next term which I might add, did not happen either. They did not make sure that the workplace understood that it wasn't Mark not wanting to turn up, but the school that insisted on it, because of some unrelated misdemeanours. That was not stated and left Mark without options. He was unable to volunteer even though he tried hard to gain volunteer work at these places, as now he was not covered by the school insurance. He was left without options at this time. However, he was very innovative in ways of creating opportunities which I will later explain.

CHAPTER 3

Growing Up

Jason had some local friendships and was at the age he could go down the creek which was on our property and about 150 metres away. Sarah and local friends all built cubby houses. Sarah would have everyone organized with a horse and ropes and build pens for the horses. Jason didn't like riding, but he wasn't frightened of being around them. Thanks to Sarah, they created imagination games for hours and I could hear from up in the house the squeals of laughter and fun as they created games and hiding and catching one another. Sometimes Jason would fish with these same friends and come home with turtles. Mandy and Mark were often unable to go with them and often stayed upstairs as I felt they were too young to go down without adult supervision. Mandy would ask if she could go down with them too by saying "me too, me too". My response would be "no you're not old enough yet". She would say "I are too". We started calling her "Me2 I R2".

I remember one year Jeff wanted to clean out the dam as it had a lot of sediment in it and it was nearly dry. He decided to pump the rest of the water out. The dam had only been there for 3 years at this time. The kids, inspired by Sarah, found some eels; now I can't remember how they caught them, but I do remember there was a bathtub outside which had been a trough. It now was the home for about 50 filthy, slimy, slippery eels. I was not impressed!!! They thought it was great!

Now was the time I started work, just when Mark had started school. I had odd hours working at an aged care facility. I also started working at the piggery at the same time as both jobs were part time. Mark would sometimes visit the aged care facility and the older residents loved him helping out. It was a great job, but I often wouldn't get home on time and Mandy was at an age that I think she started to feel she wasn't getting the attention and interest from her mum, so I decided to leave the aged care facility and I was offered permanent work at the piggery. It did give me better hours to be home for the kids after school.

Mark and Jason were very involved in our local community through the Tiaro church and school activities. Even when we moved later to Maryborough, everyone knew and loved them. That later turned out to be Mark's saving grace!

I remember one birthday that had past some three weeks earlier while I was in the local paper shop, he sat outside and told everyone who would listen that it was his birthday. It was a big deal to him, still is. He then was about 7 yrs. old. One customer bought him an ice block!

While Jason was a little shy Mark was always around people and loved to talk all the time. He used many big words and it was interesting that he listened so carefully to know how to use them. He did make us laugh on occasions, as sometimes he got it wrong, but he tried and still does. He is very good with spelling too so now, if he is unclear in language, he will spell the word so that we can understand. Jason isn't so good with spelling. They both have good vocabulary and sentence construction. They both are used to repeating themselves when we don't understand and this has allowed them to explain how they are feeling and not becoming frustrated. It was always important to ask them to clarify what they were saying no matter how many times they were asked to do it, because it meant that we were interested in what they had to say, which made them feel valued. Now of course they are pretty clear. It can be a little tricky though when they use the phone as I can't see the other expressions that they use alongside their speech while on the phone. This is only when they are talking about something which is unfamiliar, but then Mark will spell the word if we are having trouble understanding, which I think is interesting because he mightn't be able to say it well, but he can spell it. If Mark is talking a lot or sometimes, I have something on my mind and my mind is being somewhere else, Mark sees my disinterest and will say "oh I know, too much talking, too much talking, sorry. Okay I'll shut up". He still does this to this day. I always smile and then it puts me back on track again to listen. He seems to have an uncanny knack for reading people who are kind to him, unless they are online, more about that later.

One day I had to prepare for a speech as I had joined Toastmasters. Now I prepared in front of the mirror, in front of Mark and I explained how nervous I was feeling. Mark, who was about nine years old, then said "Now mum you will be good at it, just think about what you want to say and just talk really slow, so it is nice and clear. Take your time". I have learnt heaps about language from these boys of mine!

As I said they were both very involved in the local community and when it came to those times when they became interested in girls as with any teen it is scary but with a person who has an intellectual disability it's scarier. I guess this is the time you have THE TALK! Jason seemed to have understood and I thought he would ask when he was ready. No need to elaborate too much all at once.

It wasn't long before Mark found a lovely girl who also had Downs Syndrome at school. He was smitten, he loved her long hair and her charm, and he even kept her photo under his pillow! It was particularly hard because Mark and his girlfriend wanted to have a baby because babies are so "adorable"! They were both 15 years old. Even though they were not sexually active I felt that this was coming. Mark was very good and asked a lot of questions, but the first hurdle was talking about the implications of having a baby. Now to ensure that my point was clear this happened on a daily basis. I was fraught with anxiety about this. We talked about how lovely it is to have a friendship and knowing and liking the person you're with and this might mean just talking and spending good times with that person. It could mean a cuddle or kiss or two. Sometimes that leads to feelings of wanting sex and that feeling can be overwhelming. Then I gave the TALK. I also spoke about the implications of having sex, the sexually transmitted diseases, an unplanned pregnancy and if they didn't know each other well, break ups can occur. That's even harder if you have a baby. You know when I spoke about friendships needing a third person to maintain the friendship, well, I was that third wheel! They were well chaperoned wherever they went.

Mark was good at rock n roll which I taught him. Because he was a little too short for me and made me go into some strange positions as I swung under his arms, I thought it would be good for him to have his girlfriend and him be taught together. She had already been doing ballet. He loved her so and when they got there, he would try to do the dancing, but his girlfriend would get upset and go and sit in a corner of the dance hall somewhere away from him -- continually. This happened on every occasion they went. He would really try to please her in every way and say come on let's not fight, let's dance. I'm afraid it just wasn't working Mark did everything to try and get his friend to dance but she was always upset with him. He pandered so much to her that I think that made it worse and she would hide in the toilets, etc., where he couldn't talk to her. He was so upset and he didn't understand it. He never would give up and we tried to assist but nothing worked, eventually I would say well mate she really is not being nice to you. It still took ages before he came to that realization. He was so hurt. I watched unable to help him while he went through a broken heart for the first time. He would ring her, or she would ring him, and it would always end with her saying "well I'm going out with another boy because I don't want to go out with you anymore. Virtually she would be saying things that would hurt him. Then she would ring him up again and start talking to him like nothing had happened and then finish with something else which was equally hurtful. I am not blaming her because those teenage years are hard and there is a lot of sorting out to do when it comes to relationships. Eventually Mark got jack of it and his friend would ring up when we were out and leave these very, very long messages on our phone. Mark would sometimes ring her back and again she would say something that hurt Mark. She would ring continually and eventually he would snub her and not speak to her at all, even today, years later, I can't get him to just say hello to her when passing her in the street, he just doesn't want to speak to her at all. Guess that's the way he manages the hurt, I suppose. Mark is a very social person though.

When we would go to an outing Mark had all these beautiful girls talking to him. He was quite cute sitting on a seat with a number of older girls (in their twenties while he was about 12 or 13 years old) enthralled with what he was saying. I remember when we were at such an outing and Shane (our son in law) was holding his newborn baby (our grandchild) and walking with Mark. Mark stopped and started talking to these gorgeous looking girls. When Shane came back, he said "I'll be darned, I'm sticking with him; he gets to have more chicks surround him than I do and I'm carrying my cute baby!!"

And with that came Mark's lack of insight. He thought he could go on a date with anyone, Elle McPherson, or any beautiful girl or some great singer like Madonna. He used to ask how he could meet her and ask her out!! He felt he didn't have a disability and he could ask anybody out and he soon became very disappointed. He was quite insistent and didn't take no for an answer very well. He would come up with some really out there options on how it could happen. For an example when he found and became friendly with a local girl who was married, he thought it would be good if he lived with both of them together – and told them so.

Limitations to the boys' understanding made it difficult and I never was sure how much they understood correctly. I didn't want them to be hurt. I would try to explain that beautiful girls would have lots of boys who were friends. If he was to go out with someone it is best to get to know them from the inside, from their heart. I said that beautiful and good-looking girls often have all these boyfriends who have no disabilities and I'm sure they would like him as their friend because he was so nice on the inside, but they would be looking for a boy without disabilities. This was hard as I didn't want them to be hurt any more than they were going to be. I encouraged them to look at someone who might have a disability themselves and I named a couple of girls. I said to Mark that he could still have a crush on the other stars, because that's pretty normal, but they probably wouldn't go out with him just like there were boys that wouldn't go out with me before I was married because I was too tall, to old, or not their type, or too something. It is just the way it is. I said I was sure he would find someone nice and not to aim too high just try to have lots of friends. He was quite prejudiced about someone with disabilities. We talked about we didn't see his disabilities, we saw him for the person he was on the inside, we saw his heart. Most people will have something about them that's not perfect. It's part of being human. I tried to influence him to look at the person's character.

At this time, Jason was heavily involved with his Karate and ten pin bowling. He loves these activities very much. He stuck at karate for 15 years and eventually with the help of good instructors, he became a black belt. Wow was that worth celebrating!!

There were no exceptions because of his disability, he won it fair and square, but they spent the time with him to encourage and nurture his passion. As a mother I found it difficult to watch when he fought in a competition. He used to have to fight to go up a grade. Now Jason, in his earlier years, used to go unconscious when he fell e.g., playing on a jungle gym. The doctor had explained that it was because when he fell his brain would become jarred momentarily, but it was not properly investigated, and he grew out of it. It was a worry though at the time, as I wasn't sure if he would snap back into consciousness, even though it was always only brief, usually only a couple of seconds. Anyway, it had not happened now for years when he started fighting and doing Karate. Also, it is more common for people with Downs Syndrome to have a problem with their necks called atlantoaxial subluxation. This atlantoaxial subluxation or AAI can include abnormalities of the ligaments that maintain the integrity between the first (C-1) and second (C-2) cervical vertebrae or can be related to bony abnormalities of either or both of these vertebrae. It doesn't always cause symptoms, so x-rays are important if the person is going to participate in gymnastics or sport. The instability is recognized through lateral neck radiographs where the excessive mobility of C-2 to C-1 results in an abnormally large distance between these two vertebrae. X-rays did not reveal any of these abnormalities that would influence Jason's inability to join in these activities and he really wanted to do them. However, this knowledge did nothing to alleviate my frustrations, anxiety and concerns when he was fighting.

But when I watched a fight, I would be saying to myself 'don't hit him there -- we spent a lot of money on his teeth and oh no! ---- Don't hit him there he has had a heart condition, --- don't hit him there his head might jar, --- don't hit him there you might hurt his neck, ---- Boy if you hurt my son!'

His father took him after that!

As a matter of fact, his karate has helped his coordination and his ability to use both sides of his body because, before this time, riding a bike was so difficult for him. He could not push the pedals with the other foot when he was younger. He would try so hard, and I remember him being pushed off by Jeff as he learned to ride his bike only to get a couple of feet before the bike and Jason were on the ground. He did this over and over and over again and I remember asking him if he was finished riding his bike and his reply was "yeah, I'm too sore".

After starting karate, he was able to do these things. We had spent a lot of time teaching him to ride his push bike, but it was karate that made the difference. It gave him balance. He just loved it.

He was very proud of himself when he was asked to go up on stage on Disability Week and give a Karate demonstration. Mark had started karate although he did not do karate for long, but at this time, he was a yellow belt, so he joined him on stage as Jason needed another person on stage to show off his skills. Now my chest was filled with pride as my boys went up on stage and Jason was doing his carter and showing his moves and knowledge; Mark -- not so much. My pride waned into dismay and those lovely feelings were replaced with horror as I watched the two boys start to argue and then really get into a fight. "You shouldn't have done that Mark" Jason had said with a reply of "you don't know, cause I'm learning it too" and punches started flying everywhere. I had to slink up on stage, very embarrassed to try and stop the fight, while they had an audience of about 80 people laughing!

When Jason learnt to ride his push bike, a few other neighbourhood kids, whom were his friends, came over to see if Jay wanted to go with them riding their bikes. How could I say no? The condition was they ride down a very quiet road near our place towards the river or the bottom of our farm as the road went around the circumference of our place. Although a frontage was on the highway he wasn't allowed to go there. The boys could avoid this. Jason knew his road rules and was always made to wear a bike helmet while the other boys did not. Fortunately, he was wearing one when he was thrown into the air by the bonnet of a car which was only going very slow. Jason had no injuries thankfully. Jason tends to look directly in front of him and not ahead down the road. He had become good on his bike and while he was with the others, we thought he would be relatively safe. About a year later the boys went on their bikes to our small town of Tiaro avoiding the highway by riding on the quiet road around the back of the town. However, they had to cross the highway to get to the other side and down the back paddocks. The others had crossed the highway but when it came to Jason's turn, he crossed the highway not by walking, but riding his bike and again he was hit by a car. We were called and also the ambulance. The ambulance thought there were no significant injuries, but they would take him to hospital to check him out. Jason was minimally complaining about his sore arm and his nose. We also know that Jason has an extremely high threshold for pain so if he complains about something being sore it probably was broken which is what happened in his case. His arm was fractured, and his nose had a hairline fracture. It all mended well and when it came time to go with the boys riding again, I asked him whether he thought it was a good idea to ride again on the road. His reply was simple "oh no mum, I'm sick of being a Speed Bump!" I'm so thankful for his insight and his good sense of humour. His high threshold for pain was also evident when he was very young and was playing over at the neighbour's place. He was spiked by her garden edging which was made of cut reinforcing steel. It was stuck in his leg about 10 mm or half an inch, and he was unable to move. He was not complaining just sitting and waiting until someone got there. He went to hospital for a tetanus injection. It healed well too.

Before Jason could balance and ride his bike Jeff thought it would be good for Jason to have a go at riding a scooter (in our paddock). He seemed to have an ability and so he didn't miss out, we bought a motor scooter which was 80cc step-through. Jeff spent ages and converted it to three wheels. Jason loved that scooter and he became very capable on it although he thought it only had one gear – second – we thought it was safer that way.

As Jason grew older, he became very capable of mowing the grass with the proper safety gear on, of course, but only the front yard as it didn't have too many obstacles and it was a large, very flat area. We had just put a campervan in the front yard and went out. So, when we came home, we noticed the caravan had been shifted. We were guessing that the neighbour had shifted it on Jason's insistence so he could mow around it. Oh no! Jason informed us that he had towed it with his little scooter!! Talk about problem solving!! The neighbours had watched on from their kitchen window because they thought how ingenious he was, and they didn't want to stop him.

He was capable of many things. Remembering that there were not many cars on the road back then and Jason always wanted to obtain his license. He nagged us. Even though we knew his reaction time was slow we didn't want to destroy his confidence. We told him not to be disappointed if he couldn't get his license as it was very hard and it was extremely important because someone including himself could get hurt or killed if he did the wrong thing. We said we felt that he may not get the license because he may not understand all the rules and his reaction time was a bit slow and a lot of people can't get their license. We mentioned his accidents with his bike. Anyway, that didn't influence him, and we got him a book to go over all the rules of the road. We said that if he could learn the learner's booklet and go for his learners and he passed that we would pay for him to have a teacher and do a defensive driving course until he got his license. I remembered the professor so many years ago saying, "and why can't a person who has Downs Syndrome be a bus driver"? Very determined Jason spent many hours and weeks learning that car learner's booklet. He tried so hard to learn it. So, when he felt he knew it and was ready, I decided to ask him some questions from the booklet. I asked them and he would've got 100% right except that I asked them out of order that they were in the booklet. He had learnt the answers rote and in order of the booklet. He did not comprehend the relevant answers to particular questions. He knew all the answers but not in relation to the question only in relation to what number they were! So not to be discouraged, we offered for him to drive the old ute around the paddock, as long as he had one of us in the ute. He did this often, but it was he who came to the realization that it was too hard to go for his license. He drove really well in the paddock until we asked him to break. His reaction time was slow and he had no perception of space. He could not anticipate where or how close an object was or how wide the vehicle he was driving was. This made for some very interesting drives, and I soon learnt to give the job to his father, too nerve racking for me!! His life was full, but he would have to rely on others to get him from A to B. This was a bit of a problem living on the outskirts of town with no public transport and wanting him to be as independent as possible. He had a job in the piggery which is way out of town. More about that later.

However, a little later on, Jason did manage to get his boat license. Yes, a boat license, he tried so hard to get that boat license and he had a really good carer to support him. This carer, Gary, who supported him in community access, had a contact who was a licensed teacher. This teacher spent a few days helping Jason out on the water to understand and know the safety issues and rules. He came home sporting his boat license – wow what an achievement. How proud we felt! He now could take the helm, oh, I forgot to mention, Jason bought himself a boat and now he could steer it! He could also afford a car but while he finally got his boat, Jason always needed someone to take him to the water as he didn't have his drivers' license.

Jason still loves his ten-pin bowling and he often went away with this bowling group. He went to Tasmania to represent Maryborough. Now I have to say here that there was opposition on letting him start ten-pin bowling because well-meaning people said that "you take them on a bus with all the others who have a disability. It's putting him in a pigeon hole and making him stand out. Why not let him join a league without people with disabilities". Now my point is lots of people have opinions, but I could see that Jason loved his bowling, even today, he is very good at it too. He has maintained friendships from this activity and feels like he belongs with people who don't judge him. He has some really good friends. I know I would feel solace in a garden club or Toastmasters, people with same interests who don't make me work and try so hard to keep up with the rest of them, just allowing me to relax and enjoy the moments. Anyway, in a "normal" setting would he gather good friendships and a beautiful girlfriend (now his wife) like he has done in this team? Likely not.

Mark didn't find any of these activities appealing and I think that it was good that Jason had his own activities and adventures he participated in. There were no shadows here and Jason soon developed into a man to be proud of and you know what, Jason is proud of himself too with good self-esteem and self-confidence.

One of Jason's passions was swimming and going out fishing. I must say that Jason is an extremely good swimmer and he loves it. I remember all of us going down to a river and Jason would swim under water for such a long time. We would get worried because the water was murky, and we couldn't see him readily. But he was like a dolphin and would come up for air eventually. As far as his fishing, alas I don't think we took him out fishing enough. He bought his own boat, and he was very keen. His support worker, Gary would take him. But when this worker left to start his own business, Jason just didn't get out on the water much. He eventually sold his boat. It is here I need to mention that Jason made a deal with a bloke whom he worked with at the piggery, to buy the boat. Shall we say it was not in Jason's best interests, so we had to step in? It was a bit like stepping on glass because we didn't want Jason to feel he hadn't done well or to put him on the outer with his mates at work. More about work later. Anyway, we renegotiated, and Jason sold his boat for a much better price.

Both boys found what activities they liked. Mark loved Rock n roll and he soon had all the really good dancers dancing with him when we went out. He would just rock up and ask them. It was interesting to see because they would not usually dance with anyone else bar their partners. Here he seemed to always get a yes and really enjoyed himself, showing off to everyone. He would dance with me also, but I did find it difficult especially when he would ask for a complicated move and I was towering nearly a meter taller than him. I remember fondly when we were out and he would ask Melody to dance. One of the moves he had learnt was to kneel on one knee and flip her rock n roll skirt out as she went around and around. It was a move he learnt from a rock n roll teacher, Mervin when he and his girlfriend went to their rock n roll beginners' group. Must have been the one time his girlfriend wasn't mad with him! He would always ask Melody to dance and she always did. She is such a beautiful dancer and entered into many a competition dancing, and that's why many people were not game to ask her, --- except you know who!

Mark spent many a night with us dancing until he turned 18 years old. He still went with us and would say that he would get the bus home instead of waiting for us. We thought this was good for his independence until that night we couldn't find him. As we lived away from the boys by this time on a farm 50 kms away we didn't check every night if Mark got home safely as the

Sports club bus took him right to the door which was about 3 kms from the Sports Club. Jeff and I had been staying with them until we bought this farm. Because Mark was living with his brother Jason; Jeff and I would often just carry on back to our farm. I just had a feeling this one night, so we went home to check on him. He just seemed too eager to get home. When we got to his home, he wasn't there. I didn't know what to do. I rang the Sports club and as they were about to close, I was lucky to get an answer. The staff said that they had been talking about going to the Criterion known as the Cri. I have to say here that Jeff was a little bit annoyed at me, but I really wanted to know where he was. I had my hot pink jeans on and leather black jacket along with my hair in a ponytail and a bright pink ribbon in my hair (I was dressed for rock n roll). Now I went inside the Cri and there he was having a great time but very vulnerable because I could see he was being a little bit of a nuisance there when people didn't want to associate with him, he wouldn't accept that. I really wanted him to come home as he had just turned 18 yrs. old and still very young in so many ways. Well Mark had different ideas! So, I told him that I would stay until he changed his mind. I sat on this big lounge in the foyer with all my attire and waited. Now there were teeny boppers everywhere so can you see a picture of this big old momma sprawled out on the lounge at the entrance of the 'Cri'. I think I might have looked like I was waiting for a pick up! I thought the bouncer would have come and moved me on. Mark eventually decided he'd better come home – but it was about 15 mins later. I think I might have been an embarrassment to him! He found out that I, too, can be, well -- determined. I tried to explain to Mark what he needed to do and if he really wanted to go then he had to obey certain rules. We went through them with Mark, but we wasted our breath because Mark loved to find boundaries and blur them a little. He was drinking too much and he is not nice and very vulnerable when he is drunk. Thankfully he grew out of this stage but before he did, we had many incidences. He was determined to go again so we tried to explain to Mark his vulnerabilities, safety aspects and what he needed to do. He had certain rules he needed to follow so we weren't so worried and also to ensure he was safe. We asked that he always prearranged a bus or cab home and talked about safety; that he came home at a decent hour, 12 midnight, that he didn't drink too much and what that meant. We also explained that he could be too "clingy" with people and not give them any space. I wanted to make sure that Mark knew the difference from a person being friendly and his known friends. A person being friendly doesn't mean they're your friends. He always had trouble with this difference. All these rules had to be discussed to ensure his understanding was the same as ours. I was terrified as we knew those boundaries were about to be tested! What he didn't know was that we had spies everywhere. I know many people in Maryborough (some through work) and as I found out later many of them went to the 'Cri'.

We asked Mark that when he went to the Cri, he had to get a taxi home. I would make sure he had money. Now Mark has ways of blurring the boundary lines and to get home from the Cri he subsequently organized the security man, or friends that we knew by telling them he couldn't get home. However, they were becoming knowing and it didn't always work. Mark walked home a couple of times. He was also mixing his drinks and drinking too much. One night or should I say early one morning (no he didn't keep the curfew either) he was walking down the road and obviously had too much to drink. He was wobbly. A friend of ours was about to start his shift in the garbage truck when he saw Mark. He went and picked him up in his own vehicle and drove Mark home. We were at a loss at how to solve this and Mark's safety was in jeopardy. We spoke to him, we stayed over at their place in Maryborough thinking that if he thought we were monitoring him, he might comply more, hah! We took him out to the farm a lot more hoping he'd participate in the set boundaries, then he could stay in town. He still found innovative ways of not complying and not telling the truth. It was very worrying times. Jeff and I spoke to a friend who we know very well, knows nearly everyone in town and who is very caring of the boys. We stated that it sounds awful but if Mark had got a fright or got worried about his safety, he might comply better to our wishes as we didn't want him hurt. It wasn't long after that talk, that Mark didn't go out anymore and when he did, he didn't drink too much and got home on time. We knew something had happened but we just don't know what. Nor did we find out, nor did we want to. But whatever works!

I remember when he went to another pub and found some people whom he liked and who were friendly to him. He didn't know them but Mark thought they seemed friendly enough. Mark would have quickly categorized them as his friends. They kept buying him drinks and lots of different types of alcoholic drinks. It was becoming a bit of fun for them to see Mark walking all over the place and talking all jumbled up. At this time an off-duty policeman (yes, we know them too) came into the bar and saw this happening. He went up to the barman and said that if he served Mark another drink, he would ensure that he would have his liquor license revoked. The cop knew Mark and got him a taxi home. It didn't matter where he went, he would always meet someone who would keep him safe. He and our family seem to be well known either through friends or acquaintances, Mark and his escapades (more likely) or from where Jeff or I had worked or danced. The cops were also protective and let me know what was going on and if there were things, they had concerns about. When I'd say to Mark that I heard about what he did the other night, he would say "How do you know mum". My reply was always "a little bird told me, or mothers' know everything".

Mark loves music so one day I gave him a treat and we went to see Graeme Connors, the singer who was playing live on stage at the Brolga in Maryborough. Mark had already seen him in Bundaberg about one year before. He loved the show so much and sung along to the music he knew so well. As he did in his previous shows, Mark went to line up after the show to get Graeme's autograph and talk to him. When he finally got to talk to him and get his autograph, Graeme said, "oh, my mate Mark from Maryborough". Mark was thrilled. He had his photo taken with Graeme too. Mark loved that and he felt quite special in front of the crowd. At another singer's concert we went to, the drummer took him out the back and gave Mark some drumming sticks. People can be really nice especially in our smaller community. Thank you, Maryborough!

It's not all good experiences but he does find kind people around him. One occasion I remember Mark had been accosted by a boy outside Centrelink. I found out later. A few weeks later, this same boy tried it again in Station Square Shopping Centre. However, a girl (who had been bullied at school herself) saw the whole thing unfolding. This stirred something within her and she acted. Even though she did not know Mark she told the abuser off and made him apologise to Mark for bullying him.

With the help of our community Mark was keeping safe. When we didn't go to the Sports club, Mark would still go. He knew everyone there and so did we, so Mark was always enjoying himself and behaving there and I would hear about it if he wasn't. Everyone watched out for him, including staff. He had befriended the footballers who would end up at the club. I think that was when he started to drink as he always hung around them and they were very supportive of him, but they usually liked to celebrate. There were a couple of footballers who would talk with him and be very supportive of him. He started going out to watch a match when they were playing football on the weekends. He would run out with the water for them. They called him "the water boy". He was very proud of his nickname and his duties. But there was nothing more special when one night at the Sports club when the footballers went out onto the dance floor and were standing there together singing with the live band a song they knew. I can't remember what it was called. They lifted Mark up on their shoulders while they sung. Mark had the most beautiful, proudest expression and smile on his face. Wow! And me -- well I had tears in my eyes.

CHAPTER FOUR

Incidents

In 2003 we bought a new car, a Prado. The whole family was so happy to finally get a brand-new car. With a new car I tend to become pedantic in cleaning it and keeping it tidy. At least we were! We were still living in Tiaro and Maryborough town was about 20 minutes away. Jeff had gone down the paddock and I decided to go into town shopping in the other car. I wasn't worried about the kids they were older now, and Mark was 15 years old. Jeff was around and our neighbours were home, so I went. Mark decided he would surprise us and wash the car for us but he wasn't sure how to get it out of the garage. He decided he could reverse it out so he could wash it ---and anyway driving looks easy doesn't it! He's short so I'm not sure he could even see above the steering wheel, and he was probably looking down at his feet on the pedals trying to work out which one did what. We had a large garden in the middle of the driveway which acted as a roundabout for the cars to go round. It has very large boulders around it and trees in the middle. The garden stood about 45 centimetres from the ground. Anyway, he must've found reverse and the accelerator, and with a very fast pace the car had reversed up the boulder edged garden and then into the tree in the middle of the garden. Although a young tree it did stand about 3 metres tall – well it did. Mark had reversed the car into it and pushed it over. Now realising he was in trouble he decided he needed to put the car back in the shed --- guess what he did on the way in??? Yes, he crashed the front of it as well! Now the car had damage everywhere front and back and the only solution Mark could come up with, was to put a sheet over the car, just so we wouldn't notice. He also called Jack Casey Toyota in town and asked them where he could get the car fixed. He then called Kingston's panel beaters and asked them to come out quick and fix the car up – before mum got home!!! When I arrived home, I thought it strange that there was a sheet on the car. You can imagine my surprise and horror when I lifted it. However, I had to remember why Mark did it. He wanted to help and wash the car. Hmmm!

As there was $7,500 worth of damage which was an extreme amount back then, I rang the insurance company. They said that they could pay because although he was an unlicensed driver it was in our house yard. They said we would need to pay the access of $1,500 because he was under 25 years old.

We were in a difficult situation because it was still a lot of money and we really wanted Mark to learn how much money this really was and its value because other than day to day money he had for spending, he had no idea. We decided to have him do some work for us at $10 an hour to pay off the access. Now Mark is not a very, shall we say, energetic lad so it was taking him a long time to get motivated and as he said "it takes a lot of time, doesn't it? When will it finish?" That was 20 years ago. So, if anyone knows of any community services required, he has 97 hours left! No really, we did wipe the debt some time ago as he got the message and has *some* understanding how much that money is worth.

Jason had started working at the local hardware store by now. We had an employment agency support him, but it wasn't working for him and when the firm spoke to me, they said that Jason was getting paid full casual rates and doing very little for it and often had to have someone to help him. The other employees were upset, and so the employer said they would have to let him go. I was really annoyed because the employment agency should have let them know that his pay should be subsidized by the Government and if he could only work say 60% capacity then the firm would be offset by the Government for the other 40%. Also, they had a duty to stay with him until he could do the work satisfactorily or monitor him frequently and at the very least, talk to the firm. I was annoyed and got another agency to work with Jason. At this time, I was working at a local piggery and asked, with a support worker, would they consider Jason. The boss was interested and extremely tolerant. The employment agency took him to work for some time and back again as I wasn't working the same hours. As this was approximately 25 kms from home and another 25 kms for the agency to travel it was short lived and they stated that they encouraged participants to find their travel to and from work independently. However, the other reason was because the smell from the piggery was making the employment agency staff member sick to the stomach. He said one time to me that he didn't know how anyone could eat lunch there. He sat outside the sheds and couldn't help Jason at all. Anyway, the boss was really good and teed up workers who were going past our home to pick Jason up and drop him off. Sometimes the boss even ran Jason home himself if the others weren't at work. As I said that Jason's boss, Mick, was very good to Jason and none more when Jason had a little accident with the feed. Jason was filling up the barrow to feed the pigs as that's what they did then, it was done manually. He'd been shown how, so his Forman, Bob, left him in charge of feeding. Jason had trouble and came up to his Forman who was a little way away and said, "Bob what do I do with this?" Jason was filling up the feed from the silo into the barrow. He had the slide from the bottom of the silo – you know --- that slide that stops all the grain from the silo emptying – he had it in his hand!!! Bob has never run so fast!

Jason never did do that again as he and Bob had to shovel it all back. The boss, Mick was good about that too. Jason gave 100% to his job and loved doing it for 25 years.

When the boss was no longer and Jason had a new boss, it wasn't so easy and I got a phone call from the new boss soon after the boss commenced working there. He stated that they had just done a workplace and safety audit and it was advised that Jason was deemed unsafe in this environment because of all the trucks and grain being carted. There had already been an accident many years earlier where a person had the grain emptied over him and nearly died except for the quick-thinking staff who dug him out. They would have to let Jason go. Jason had been working there about 15 years at this time and now he was deemed unsafe, really!

Well now you know those assertive techniques I had learnt; he was about to find out for himself how good they'd become! I began by saying that Jason had worked there a long time without incident. I stated that if they were concerned keep him away from that area. I also stated that while Jason had an intellectual impairment, he was very safety conscious and if they went through the rules with him or asked him about the rules, he would give good account. I said it sounds like you have made an assumption without knowing him, in fact it sounds very much like discrimination to me. I asked that they give him a go and then see what they think. The magic word was "discrimination", and he was given a go. I rang the boss up 1 month later to see if he felt differently and he was so full of praises of Jason's work ethic, never having time off and giving 100% to the job. He said he loved the tasks that were boring to others because he knew what to do and the task didn't change. He said, "I wish all my workers were like that!" That's our son!

Jason worked for many more years there and had been saving well. As Jeff and I were selling our home and moving west of Maryborough it was best for Jason to live in Maryborough where he could get lifts easily to work. He saved up and proudly bought himself a home in Maryborough. Jeff and I stayed with him for some time to get him into a routine. We lived there but moved in and out to our other home when it was required. I also worked in Maryborough, so it was making life easier all round. Jason continued to tee up lifts himself, but sometimes he had trouble because someone wasn't working or just didn't turn up without bothering to tell Jason. This made Jason look irresponsible. Work for Jason now was about 90 kms from our farm house and that was just one way! We often had to take him to work at the last minute, rushing to get him there when a worker didn't turn up with a lift. One day he rang David from his address book to take him to work. Wrong David as this one lived some 150 kms away. We had used him for our saddlery. When we found out we put all the workers' names and phone numbers in one part of his address book in the order for him to start ringing. This worked better, but he still had the odd lift who didn't let him know if they weren't going to work. I rang the person who continually didn't let Jason know. I asked him if he could let Jason know if he wasn't going to work, as Jason used to wait out on the steps half an hour before his lift was due to come and if he didn't show, he would wait another half an hour later. This wasn't fair. It can be awfully cold outside at 4:30 am on a winter's morning waiting one hour for nothing. Seemed to improve after that and after all Jason was paying his way which I thought was a little bit too much money for his lifts but he didn't have a choice. Anyway, he still had enough money to pay his mortgage and food and fun money he didn't need to go without. He would have spent more if he had his own car with maintenance, etc.

It was this time that Jason decided to rent a place at Tiaro through the week to maintain his lift opportunities. It was also Sarah and Shane's house so his rent was cheap. He would return home on week-ends to his own house and Mark. The Tiaro house was a half way point to work. He would get his lift on Mondays, drop his gear off, stay the week, until Friday when he'd come back to his home. This was relevant because there were workers from the piggery living in Tiaro. This gave him more chance to reliably get to work and get a lift. Mark stayed by himself through the week and Jason would be there on weekends. I received a phone call from Fraser Coast Family Networks saying that someone had seen Mark walking down the highway, on the outskirts of Tiaro with a large bag in his hands. I do have spies everywhere! I rang him, he did not answer. I thought I'd better go after him. I rang him again and he answered saying he was going to spend the week with Jason. He just hadn't told anyone. How did he get there some 25 kilometres from Maryborough? Well apparently, he had got a lift with a friend. He told them he was going to his brother's place and they let him off in Tiaro as he requested. It was only a short walk to the house.

Mark was paying rent to Jason as he was staying in Jason's house in Maryborough so it seemed to work out well --- so it seemed! Mark was alone a lot more and had more time for those idle hands, even though we visited often. Remember I said that Mark understands how much money is worth now, well I was very surprised when I got a call from the bank. You see Mark spends a lot of time writing words to songs, recipes, and stories. He just loves it, so I didn't think anything strange about the length of time he was taking in the last couple of weeks writing happily away until I received this phone call from the bank. When I went down there, they said that they had a problem with Mark's transactions and could I come down. I was a little alarmed, but the penny still didn't drop. When I got there, Mark had taken off and the teller proceeded to tell me that Mark had come into the bank 3 times and took small amounts out to buy different items from the shops. They were only menial amounts to purchase what he wanted. He was chatty and the third time he withdrew money, he told the teller "Oh my brother lets me do this". When questioned they found that he was using Jason's bank card and signed Jason's signature. She showed me the signature and it was a perfect match! He must have been practicing for weeks!

I know the bank said it was okay, but I was concerned. If he got away with this, it might be someone else he could do it to, and after all it was 'Fraud'! I went to the police station to talk to a policeman about giving Mark a lecture. I met a policeman, (I shall call him "Gavin") at the station. I told him the story and my request by adding "you don't look scary enough". I wanted Mark to be bought to the realization of the consequences of stealing and forgery in which he was delving. Although Mark has good problem-solving skills he is very easily led and insists on impulsive decision making. Gavin said, "I have my ways, bring him in". Luckily Mark had gone home, and I told him the police wanted to talk to him. He said he wouldn't go so I explained that a policeman would come to the house and pick him up if he didn't. With that he came willingly.

We arrived at the station and 'Gavin' came straight out. Mark wanted me to go in with him, but I refused telling him he was on his own and that I was annoyed with him. Mark had just turned 18 years old. Gavin returned 10 minutes later and explained what he was doing. He told Mark that he'd talked to me, and he was going to say to him that we didn't want to have someone who lies and cheats and steals money at home now and that it was a criminal offence. When 'Gavin' got back Mark had his arms folded in front of him and said, "anyway I'm 18 now you can't touch me". 'Gavin' responded with "18 hey, oh that's really bad. I'll have to talk to (we'll call him) Warren. You could go to jail for an offence like this – this is fraud and stealing and that you could go to jail for 10 years". He asked Mark how many times did he do it and Mark told him, "Once". He repeated the question and Mark said, "once". The sergeant said "Well, the bank told me it was a lot more than that. How many times?" Mark replied that it was about 6 times. He obviously had been making a career out of it because I did not know this. 'Gavin' said "that's 6 times 10 years that's a lot of years in jail. You could be 78 yrs. old before you would get out!!!"

With that 'Gavin" picked up the phone and asked "'Warren' have you got a cell for a young offender for the night". Mark's eyes widened and 'Gavin' said that he would need to go down to the watch house. 'Gavin' took him down and Mark just sat there without any doors closed behind him. 'Gavin' said that he would check with mum to see if I'd changed my mind. 'Gavin' waited with me for about 2 minutes and said "that should do him. I'll tell him he can come home if he apologizes and promises not to do it again." Mark's attitude had changed and after initially apologizing he hugged and clung to me. We walked out like we were in a three-legged race, he hugged me so tightly and he wasn't letting go. When Mark got into the car, he turned to me and asked solemnly "Mum is that where they have the electric chair?" I was trying hard to stifle my laughter. I just couldn't. Later I went and thanked "Gavin" and Mark has never done that again.

There has been a lot of trials and lots of funny things happen along the way as life throws its curve balls and I wouldn't miss them for the world!

However, there were a couple I could have done without, although they did turn out humorous, because, while that scenario could have been quite serious, there was a comical side to it all.

As I said there have been some great times. Mark has a good heart and loves people. Oh, I didn't tell you, Mark is a great massager and whenever we have the time, he massages my feet or brushes my hair. It is truly heavenly, he's a real treasure. There have been many treasures along the way, and one I remember well, when it was Jeff and my wedding anniversary. I always did special things for our anniversary, so Mark thought he would follow suit. He rang me while I was at work which was about a kilometre away. He knew where I was physically but couldn't relay it back in words to anyone, the number and street. It was our 25th wedding anniversary and it was school holidays. That is one trouble we had, we couldn't find any care for Mark and Jason back in those days. No one we knew was able to help and at that time we were unable to get support of any kind. Mark stayed at home a kilometre from my work and we checked in often. On this day Mark rang me at work and said I had to come home quick. When I asked if he was alright? He said "yeh, yeh mum, you gotta come home quick". Being assured there was nothing wrong I said I would, when I was able and I wouldn't be long. But I smelt a rat.

I got home and there was Mark very excited on my arrival, jumping up and down on the spot --- so very excited. There was a bouquet of flowers waiting for me. He said, "happy anniversary mum". Talk about ingenuity – this lad had looked up the phone book (which I didn't know he knew how) and ordered a cab, (which I didn't know he knew how) and asked the taxi to take him to a flower shop (which he didn't know where). As he didn't know where a flower shop was, and he couldn't give the taxi an exact address of my work he asked for the flowers to be delivered back to home. Hence, I was called. The flowers were delivered to him, so he rang me quickly when he received them. He is so thoughtful and that was a lovely anniversary present, bless him, this was all off his own back and he was able to follow through with his problem solving.

It was very difficult at that time to be working and ensure that the lads were safe and occupied, plus ensure the girls got time to themselves as well and, in hindsight, I could have done that better. At the time I did what I could do. I was also studying. This made it difficult for the girls and some reliance was bestowed on them to help with babysitting the boys.

Eventually Mark did get a job where I was working at the time and that was at Fraser Coat Family Networks. He used to clean the rubbish bins out and odd jobs around the office. He was not very interested in the work but mainly did it to get some money and we really wanted him to gain some work experience and acquire some ethical standard about working. Mark was putting paper through the shredder when Mark remarked about something he'd read from these papers. These papers had information that was confidential in nature. Mark's limited understanding of the word 'confidential' is a little different to our given explanation and we knew he wouldn't be able to help himself. So that job was taken away from him. While he was working there, he found a brochure on university courses. It was with great surprise and amusement that the boss witnessed Mark ringing up a Melbourne University (he was ringing from Maryborough Qld) about a course and asked that they send information on becoming a doctor. He did receive it too but he soon realised he wouldn't be able to understand it. The boss said to me one day that he didn't employ Mark for his working ability but more for his entertainment value!

Mark later got a job in a restaurant. They were really good to Mark, and he learnt many skills. We went one day with friends and Mark served us. He wrote down our orders and he was very quick. I asked if he was sure he got it right. He explained that he had abbreviations, he wrote what they taught him, and it was spot on. He attended not only to our table but other tables with equal enthusiasm and friendliness. He loved that job and was there for quite some time. He was good at it. Many people would stop me in the street and say how they only went there because Mark made them feel so special. They would say to me "He's made my day". Many reports came in about this and finally he appeared to be happy and found his 'niche'. Unfortunately, they sold this business, and the new owners didn't want to employ Mark. He was so upset. He wanted to go and talk to them and maybe I should have encouraged him to do that. The old owners bought a coffee shop and decided to keep Mark on. He would deliver coffees around town by walking to the offices and I know from reports from others that he was bewildered about where he was delivering and the delivery address, more than once. I never heard complaints, but I guess some people may have got cold coffee and some may have been surprised to see a young gentleman giving them --free coffee! He became quite bored with this work when they weren't delivering anymore. He kept saying he wasn't learning anything, and he had to fold up cardboard stands which he just didn't want to do. He begged to leave but we said that he could, if he found other work. In retrospect we shouldn't have done that as it was only then that Mark started blurring boundaries so that they would ask him to leave. As I said the owners were very good to him, so they were disillusioned and upset with Mark as his attitude had changed. He just didn't want to work there anymore, and he didn't know how to get out of it. They asked him to leave after he stole some money. He hurt them so badly they didn't want to talk to him, even when he gave the money back. Mark finally understood he did the wrong thing and felt outcast. He tried to apologise many times, but they weren't listening. They were very hurt, they trusted him.

It's at these times my fatigue was at its highest. Everyone around me were very annoyed at Mark, including family. I felt I had to listen to all the continual complaints about what he did was wrong; and while I was trying to set boundaries and consequences for him; some believed I wasn't. It was just that I wanted to set natural consequences, which did happen. It was up to me to pick up the pieces because Mark, while needing consequences, didn't need me to be his foe. He needed to talk things over after he thought about them for a while, someone to understand him; someone knowing that forward thinking of consequences for a person who has an intellectual disability is somewhat impossible and foreign, and because his character is a little impulsive (well actually quite impulsive) it can be an afterthought. However, we have always encouraged him to think of the consequences. He did need to have someone by his side but also let him know what he did was wrong. Unfortunately, I felt like I was standing alone with no-one standing by me. I didn't know if I was doing the right thing, only my instinct to guide me. I think because I stand by Mark no matter what; he has great trust in me and does listen to me, and usually tells me everything eventually, though, he can be determined or perhaps we should say here (stubborn) with other people. The other point here is that he does not respond to lengthy explanations; he will turn off; so simple and few words is best and then perhaps say it in a different way if his comprehension is limited. And you will always know when Mark has had enough explanation as he states, "too much talking, too much talking, mum". Or "talk to the hand". That little tike!

As I said earlier there have been some very funny moments and one that I recall was when I slipped over on a small puddle on the floor. As we had a new kitten I thought and said out aloud (stupid me!) that I thought it might have been cat pee. After I mopped it up, I went to work hobbling. Mark thought I was hurt and rang 000. He gave them my number. They rang me at work to ensure I was alright and had quite a giggle as they explained to me that Mark had said that "mum has hurt herself when she slipped over in some cat pee!" When I went home, I explained to Mark what an emergency is and when to ring 000. I got a call from 000 again the next day. They explained this time with even more laughter that Mark had rung to apologise! I guess that gave 000 some light relief!

When I started working in Hervey Bay, we were running a group for people who had mental health issues. We did lots of fun things that Mark would also enjoy. Mark had come to the group a couple of times when there were some interesting and appropriate activities. He loved the people and they loved him. Raymond was particularly nice to him, and they hit it off very well. Mark invited himself to Raymond's home, and Raymond said that maybe one day he could come over. I received a phone call from Raymond who said he hadn't been home but when he got there, he found Mark wondering up and down his street with 2 large bags, a pillow and a tennis racquet. He left his goods and chattels on the corner while he walked and enquired at different houses. Raymond had mentioned to Mark that he lived in this street but not the number. It is a very long, major street. Mark had got onto the bus from Maryborough to Hervey Bay intending to live with Raymond. He didn't tell anyone, least of all Raymond.

Mark was always full of surprises. Not to discount innovations. Talk about thinking outside the square! One day Mark was to meet his carer and the carer was going to take him down to Hervey Bay to our group and stay with him. We were all going to the beach and then lunch. The carer was running late and Mark didn't want to miss anything, so he did the only thing he could. He got a taxi! Now Hervey Bay is about 36 kilometres from his home. It cost over $60! It was his money I suppose. The carer rang saying he couldn't find Mark. I explained he was with me and what had happened. I told him jokingly, "that will teach you not to be late!" the carer came down and organized to spend time with Mark until I finished work. Mark loved the day, but he was broke for a while. After that he rang the staff and asked if they could pick him up, 36 kms away! Sometimes I would bring him to work because we were going to have the group for most of the day. Mark flitted around the office and was quite happy doing the paper shredding for them while he waited.

CHAPTER FIVE

Holidays

We went for a holiday with Mark to the Winton festival I can't remember the year, but Mark was only little. It was great. We stayed at a caravan park but we were next to the toilets. We were staying in a canvas pop top van. I'm here to tell you that it wasn't the toilets that smelt. Artesian water stinks and it certainly wafted into our pop-top. The owner said it was alright to drink, she said that as a matter of fact she fed it to her babies because "no self-respecting germ would live in it". We did the tourist thing and saw the Waltzing Matilda Centre before it burnt down. We also went to the old picture theatre which was open air and had canvas deck chairs or squatters' chairs. They put on an old silent movie and some old adverts like the pears soap one. It was interesting. That night before the festival was to commence, we went to a pub for tea. Mark was smitten by a girl playing the saxophone. She called herself "the Saxy Girl". Mark sat down beside her while she played. She was very kind to him actually, all the locals were. We met a lady whose name was Roslyn and her husband. They owned the mechanic's garage and he was an RACQ responder. They had lost a daughter who had disabilities some years earlier and Roslyn took a special shine to Mark. The next day they had the celebrations. Mark learnt to crack a whip, very well I might add. He would run off talking to people. There were many tourists in town. The moment came when we couldn't see him! We looked everywhere. I was starting to panic. Jeff and I separated down each side of the street because now the floats were driving down the street. Then I heard "Hello mum". I looked up and there he was. Roslyn had put Mark on top of a float for advertising their mechanic's garage. She said she had looked for us but couldn't find us. He was so happy, and we were so relieved. When it was time to leave Winton, Roslyn had promised to send Mark a tee-shirt with the mechanics logo on it. True to her word, a couple of weeks later he received a shirt in the mail.

I always had fond memories of the kindness of all the locals and really wanted to go back some day. We did, quite some years later. Jason had time off work at the piggery, so we took Jason as well. He wanted to see the dinosaur trail with their skeletons and stories. He has a fascination for dinosaurs. This time when we went back it was different, because we had to park at the racetrack, come show grounds where everyone was now designated. It was full but not only with people, the flies were disgusting. Even my dog had to wear a fly net over her head. But this time, Roslyn's husband had passed away and she had retired but still heavily involved in the local community. The Waltzing Matilda Centre had been rebuilt so we checked it out. Mark saw Jessica Mauboy (his favourite singer) live on stage. He just loved it. Later we went on to Muttaburra for Jason to stand beside a dinosaur leg which stood approximately 3 metres high. Jason's eyes were as big as saucers! We did some of the dinosaur trail and went to the museum and also found some dinosaur footprints and skeletons.

Jason couldn't wait to get back to work and tell them. When he was back at work he couldn't stop talking about the dinosaurs. Actually, both lads have a desire to work and love to work. Mark had loved his restaurant job, but it didn't last forever. However, he was still very keen to work.

I later worked in Biloela. After a lot of study, I was finally getting the job I wanted, which I had worked towards, but it was just a long way away. About 4 hours from home. I needed to live in our caravan and go home week-ends. I would often ask Mark to come with me for the week. He did this many times and made friendships everywhere. He would go to the local pub where the barmaid was friendly towards him. He didn't drink, only coke (thank God), he just talked to the locals. From all accounts they enjoyed his company, I am told. But I was surprised to hear that Mark had gone to a local employment agency and made up his resume. He then proceeded to leave copies in all the businesses in the centre of town. He loved Biloela and he certainly wasn't lacking innovation and commitment. Alas, he didn't get any jobs out of it.

He eventually went to an employment agency in Maryborough and obtained work at the Sports Club for a couple of hours a week. They would support him if he needed it, so they told us. So it was to our dismay that we were later told by a Sports Club employee, that when his ex-girlfriend came in, he would go and hide (you know --- exactly what she used to do to him when they went dancing) and of course then, he didn't do his work. The employment agency was nowhere to be found and this could have been avoided if I or they had known. I thought they were supposed to talk to the employer to find out how things were going. But it got worse! Mark asked if the Sports bus could pick him up and the Sports club said to him that they would let him know. The driver would ask the boss, as this time requested was not their usual time for transporting customers. Also, Mark was a worker, not a customer. Anyway, this day Mark had rung the Sports club up early enough, but they didn't turn up or let him know. When he rang, they said they couldn't take him. Then he rang the employment agency who didn't get back to him. I was at work and when Mark was in this dilemma, he didn't know what else to do, as he had no money for a taxi, so he rang me. He was very upset because now it was right on the working time, when he was supposed to be at work, however the work was only 5 minutes away. Luckily, I was able to leave work for a moment and went in the car to pick him up and take him to work. This time he was about 10 minutes late. I picked him up in the car and as I was backing out of the drive, the employment agency girl arrived. She had got a phone call from the Sports club stating that Mark hadn't turned up. She got out of her car and blasted Mark, very rudely I might add, for being late, and I mean blasted. Really nasty and she had no idea what Mark had tried and how upset he was already. Well, my assertive skills were about to turn to aggression, and I told her what Mark had done and how ingenious and clever he had been. I then told her what I thought of their employment agency and their lack of support. While I didn't want Mark to get further upset, I left it at that -- although 'air head' may have been a word that slipped out of my mouth. I took him to work, and I left with the worker getting to the work place by herself –supposedly to be supporting him, ---finally.

Money was becoming a big issue for Mark and although he got a pension, he spent it the same day he received it, which meant that he didn't have any money for food for the rest of the week. So much for his understanding of money! He also would not pay his bills, like Telstra for his phone, electricity and lodging. He was able to also get some money from Jason, hopefully not by sinister means. As I was paying his bills to pick up all the pieces, I thought it necessary to go to QCAT and become his guardian and administrator. It was granted through the court. This means I have the right to step in and support Mark with his finances and health. Mark has opened up several bank accounts, thinking he can buy things online and not pay for them, so therefore getting into strife. I have the authority to stop that. Otherwise, I think Mark could end up seeing that policeman again. It hasn't been without its drawbacks however particularly convincing the banks: some banks don't regard the QCAT forms as enough authorisation. This is a recent event as Mark wants to send money overseas for the scammers. I have the authority to stop this, but it is going to be very time consuming, seeing all the banks. Some have said to me he has the right. Well, he now has a lot of money in the bank, and I don't want Mark to be able to access that willy nilly. He has a budget and if he wants something and he has thought about long enough, then he can ask, and he usually gets it e.g., newest, best mobile phone, computer, dog. I just don't want to see him taken advantage of. He is so vulnerable to scams. I'm sure he is on their speed dial. A little more about that later.

Chapter 6

Parties

Birthdays are very important to our lads and even today it is with childlike enthusiasm they have expectations of their birthdays and parties.

I just want to thank people who came to Mark's 25th birthday party at Hogs Breath. Mark arranged it all himself and he had 3 close friends and our daughter Mandy and her husband, and their beautiful children, our grandchildren. I must say here that Mark hasn't got close friends that are his own age, but he has the happy knack of being able to pick the people who are friendly and caring and they seem to stick by him.

One of those people "Bronco" supported him as a support carer for a number of years and they really hit it off. The fact that Mark loves music and Bronco sung and had Karaoke was beside the point. Bronco is an animated character and Mark just loves that. He hasn't supported Mark now for some time through leaving the agency, but he still came to Mark's birthday with his daughter, Taylia.

Georgina came too. Georgina had a bread shop and one day Mark wanted to help her bring in the bread. He had been doing this for many months and he felt extremely important picking up her bread very early in the mornings. He would never normally get up early in the morning but felt he was needed and was always on time to help her. He just thought she was the greatest and as I hadn't met her before that Saturday, from my observations I think he's right. As Georgina left that day, she came over to me and said, "He represents everything good in this world". Now I have a tear in my eye while writing this. You see Georgina was a great friend to Mark for many years and was an encouragement and source of positivity and kindness to Mark. She died at the time while I'm writing this book. Mark has been really upset. She will always be remembered. I think SHE represented everything good in this world.

Last but certainly in no way least is, Doris. Doris has been Mark's friend for such a long time. I'm not sure where they met but she has always come to his birthday parties and always given a little more of herself. Doris bought her camera and took photos. Not only did she take photos of family and friends with Mark, but she also put them on a disc. Everyone always goes the extra mile for Mark.

While we had a very nice lunch, I think the best was when the staff unprompted came out with a birthday cake singing happy birthday. Mark's face shone with delight. One staff who had waited on our table ended up in one of the photos, with his insistence, of course. He told me he thought she was "Hot". Mark was so happy.

Now while this party was terrific, I also get to meet Mark's friends. They had to travel from Maryborough to Hervey Bay (half an hour away) to be there. When I look back, I realise that this boy of ours has some real special skills. Not only does he find people who are kind and caring and sought them out to be his friends – long lasting friends, he also organised the whole thing! I asked him to write down all the people who were going and check with them again the day before. He did, however a couple of people just did not turn up which disappointed him. However, knowing Mark, if he had his way, there probably would have been a whole army that day. Friendships are extremely important to him.

He also received a few cards, and I had a smile on my face when he opened my mum and dad's card. They have always sent a card with some money in it but this year when he opened it, he found no money. He said "Look mum there isn't any money this time. Oh well, they must be broke!" He evaluated that one well as they indeed had been feeling the pinch.

We gave him a computer and desk for his birthday which I had bought from Qld Health. Unfortunately, its screen was not working. He had to wait until the following week before I could buy another and he could use his computer. Yes, of course, I have concerns with Mark and the computer. For good reason as you'll see later. He is extremely knowledgeable using the computer and when I clicked the mouse to show him something, he said "mum you can do it this way. You know, it's easier". It was definitely a short cut. He knows enough to get himself into trouble particularly on the internet. I have this thought that Mark will see 'and you can get one free' advertised, that he will buy with a credit card and no understanding that he will need to have money in an account first, as a way of paying for the items. Maybe he could accidentally end up on a pawn sight or something illegal and starting a whole gamut of illegal sights and activities he shouldn't delve into. The implications, oh my goodness. Anyway, for this time we had said "no" to the internet. If we had only learnt!! I was sure though that it will only be a matter of time before Mark will have a technician out installing the internet for himself, he is just too clever. One day Mark was on my computer, and I thought he was waiting for me to come and put my password in. When I came closer to him, I could see he was happily playing on it. I asked how he got into the computer without my password. He said, "oh that's easy mum" and he continued to show me. Oh boy, I think I'll learn off him and by all accounts, I better learn quickly! Oh now --- just a current update to that forecast. It didn't take Mark long --- Mark has found that he can use the internet with his mobile by going into the Shopping Centre and getting it free. This same lad who cannot count very well, just put a calculator in his hand and he becomes a wizard.

They both have their own ways of overcoming obstacles. Jason spoke to us with great pride when he was invited to go to a party with a so-called friend from the piggery. I knew this person well and explained to him that Jay may need a little bit of attention to ensure he is okay. He'd never been to a party without us before. Anyway, this party had a few people that Jeff and I and Jay knew so we thought it should be okay; I guess we can't wrap him up in cotton wool and that is a distinction that is hard to define for parents, where do you stop and start on that line. Anyway, he wanted to go and as we were leaving for Dalby, by driving some 3.5 hours away, early next morning, we thought they would bring him home at the pre-set time (midnight) and asked if his friend could do so. 'No worries' he said. 12 midnight came and went without a sign of Jason. 6 am still no Jason. I rang everyone and couldn't get anybody, we were starting to worry and then we rang another mate of his who said that when he left Jay, he was still at this other place with a couple of people. He went back and found Jason still there on his own. They had left him behind. Jason had no phone, no way of letting anyone know if he was ok or where he was. Someone left a cigarette lighter and Jay decided that he could burn his –so called mate's--- leather jacket. This was his way of overcoming his obstacle. He had nothing else to do and he didn't know how to get out of his predicament. He was left sitting there on his own while everyone else had gone. Even though Jason did do the wrong thing, I think a burnt hole in his mate's jacket was poetic justice, wouldn't you say. He got home about 9 o'clock am and we went to Jeff's mum's place in Dalby about noon. His mate complained about the hole in his jacket, well, I don't think he will be complaining to me again. When the so-called mate came into work the next day (I was also working at the piggery at that time) he went into hiding, I mean he was hiding, and I was not able to find him. It was quite funny really and I was happy to let him sweat it out for a while. Eventually I found him. I stated that "I am very disappointed in you. I trusted you to keep an eye out for Jason. I know there is quite some responsibility for you to ensure Jay is okay. Jason was looking so much to going to this party, his first party with his friend. You left him without transport, without a phone, to stay there all night by himself. He was left there hoping someone would come back or take him home. He didn't know where he was. How would you feel? You're his friend! I am so disappointed", --- and I walked off. I knew that this would mean that Jason wouldn't be invited again but some rules had to be enforced. Interestingly he was invited the very next week to go fishing with other friends. I thought thank God! After Jason had been going out fishing with these "friends" for many months, I noticed that he was spending a lot of money on these fishing trips which were only for the day. It seemed that he would go to the servo and pay for their petrol and take out $300 dollars also. He would also buy their beer --- a carton and food for them all. They shouldn't have been drinking that much in such a short time. Who the hell was driving! Now, I was really upset and you know those assertive skills again came into play. I spoke to his friends; ever so nicely; and told them that this was abuse and illegal. I tried, I really tried to be nice, so Jason wouldn't lose his friendships, but alas, I didn't quite make it. Jason was really annoyed with me and blamed me for him losing his friends. I told him if they are his friends they will come back. I tried to explain but only time healed that one for him. There was one friend of his, Ben, who stood by Jason, and I trusted him. He really did care for Jason and when Ben went anywhere with Jay, I knew everything was okay. He took him for many fishing trips and Jay was always excited and came home exhilarated, and money in tact!

Jay has always had friends that seem to stick by him, however for us we often had to monitor what was happening --- just in case --- which seemed to be prudent given some of the things we and he had already been through. He has always loved his bowling and has been ten pin bowling for many, many years. He has always had mates there, but they rarely visited him, unless we could organize it, the third person rule, 'supporting the maintenance of friendships'. Jay has always enjoyed his bowling and rarely misses going on Friday nights. We did notice he seemed to have more interest in his bowling. Five years ago, we found out why. He found the love of his life. Julie also goes to bowling where they both are in a team. They really enjoy each other's company and always get on very well. When I found out that he had eyes for Julie, I had a big gulp. We still encouraged the next step for them to meet in Station Square (outside of the bowling team environment) and have a coffee together, but it did bring a whole lot of different circumstances we had not encountered before. Our main concern was safety and contraception should they go the next step. They met often and often they were at each other's place. I had just started working away in North Queensland so my only communication with Jason was via phone. When things were starting to hot up for Jason and Julie, I thought we'd better have another one of "THE TALKS". I asked Jeff to give him the talk again as we had done many years earlier, but never sure that he absorbed it all or understood all the detail and the touchy bits. So now Jeff had to give the talk that he found extremely difficult all those years ago. I wondered how he would get on particularly since I wasn't there to help and add to the conversation as simply as possible. Next time I called Jeff he was at Sarah and Shane's (daughter and Son in Law) place and Jay was also there. I asked what he said to him. He said he told Jason to be responsible but not much else about the birds and bees. I said "really? Better hand the phone to Jay please" When Jay came to the phone, after talking about his girlfriend, I started my spiel. I asked what they had been doing and the other things happening in his world. I continued, "Jay when you have a special friend you might like spending time and talking with her and that's all, or you might even want to hold her hand or cuddle her and that's fine too. If you both feel really close and would like the relationship to go to the next level, you both might want to kiss or have sex. Jason said nothing so I asked, "Do you know what having sex means matey?" "Oh, not really mum" "Well it's when you both want to do more than cuddle and kiss and to continue on from cuddling and kissing to make love. The man has to be very thoughtful and considerate about what they both want. She may not be ready. If she is ready, then the man puts his === A loud voice came over the phone that I recognized as being my daughter's voice, Sarah, "Mum! You're on speaker phone, the whole family are all here listening" --- and I guessed -- laughing. Well, that was embarrassing!! Anyway, Jason finally got his talk off speaker phone and Jeff was around him often to ensure he understood and if he had any questions, and while my conversation was long distance, I did the same until I could get back home. Jason said he was ready to go to the next stage. We talked about what she felt. Still concerned about contraception we felt this wasn't covered well. Amanda (daughter) also went around to his house to explain about condoms and show him how to use them and answer any questions he might have. She showed him a few times using a broom handle. My concern still was mounting as I pictured Jason putting the condom on the broom handle and saying to Julie 'We're safe now'!!!

That didn't happen thankfully, and they get on very well. When they were not together, they would phone each other every day and often several times a day. What I loved to see too, was Jason being such a gentleman to Julie. He would open the car door for Julie and hold the door open for her while she got in, --- he's just like his Dad!

By this time Jason was working less hours as they said that because they had become automated, they didn't have much work that Jason could do as the machines were doing it now e.g., feeding the pigs which had been one of Jay's chores. Bringing that time down was very hard for Jason and he felt if he showed how hard he could work, they would give him more hours. They said that "Everyone just loves Jason, but we couldn't afford for him to work the extra hours when he hasn't enough to do and his work capacity is limited". They felt retraining for work machinery was out of the question. No matter what, he was going to have less hours at work. Jason was hurt and he tried to talk them into keeping his hours. Jason did not understand and was often questioning himself saying he could work harder. He said that the piggery was his life and he wouldn't know what to do. And for a while he didn't. He eventually accepted it and was going well until they rang me up one day a few years later.

The girl who rang said that Jason wasn't performing and he'd act like he did not hear what he was being told, ignoring instructions. I know that Jay goes into his own world when relaxing sometimes, but there'd been no worries for 10 years with his other boss who was being very generous in dealing with Jay. I was starting to feel like they just wanted him gone. I wondered if he needed a hearing test. His hearing tested fine. Any conversation I had with the piggery did not cut it, I did not convince them, and Jason was made redundant. He had his cognition tested too. He had declined a little. Still, that could have been stress related.

I became concerned when I saw him looking out his front windows with a cuppa, day in and day out, just staring, not doing anything and not engaging in anything. He missed his work, and it would take a lot of other activities to motivate him --- and carers from NDIS. One of the carers was a family friend and she has been a gem. Thankfully she and one other constant also became the corner stone to the lads' care. They are very skilled. In fact, although our lads have other carers too, these two carers have become like mothers to both my boys. They are very good at relaying everything that is going on to me, keeping me updated and in the loop. The boys tell them most of their secrets and plans so sometimes we need to talk and kind of reinforce things with the boys by striking from all angles.

Jason was granted an exercise physiologist through NDIS. He used to be very proud of his physique and every time he would pass a mirror, or a new person came into his life, he would lift his sleeve to show off his muscles. Sometimes when he thought no one was around, we would see him feeling and looking at his muscles. However, that had long gone years earlier and he seemed to not have any enthusiasm for anything now. He had put on a little weight also. Then along came Jake, the exercise physiologist I was telling you about, who inspired Jason and motivated him. Now there was a sparkle in Jay's eye. To this day, Jay is very motivated, and he looks great with some muscles showing in his sleeveless shirts that he choices to wear all the time now. He walks for kilometres every day. He has lost weight. He feels great and looks it. He is quite happy to show you his muscles, --- very often. The carers have had their work cut out for themselves, trying not only to teach the lads about a good diet that has fruit and vegetables in it, but cooking for themselves healthily. Slowly but surely, they are choosing the menus now with vegetables in them and sometimes the vegetables get sneaked in. Wow, I have to say two of the carers have really worked hard and long on this one, but they're getting there. They must have the patience of a saint! Mark has been their greatest challenge!!

CHAPTER 7

Love Struck

Jason had decided that Julie was the one. They had been spending a lot of time together. Now he wanted to ask her to be his wife. Jeff and I were away still. We would have loved to be there, but I couldn't be so selfish to make Jason wait; but we did get to see it on film. Jason wanted to pop the question, NOW, since he had made his mind up. He couldn't wait. Mandy thought of a good idea and asked what Jason thought. He loved the idea. First, he went with Mandy while they picked a beautiful engagement ring. He paid it off and now he was ready for the big question. Every Thursday, Maryborough has markets. In the City Hall Park, there is a woman dressed in the 1800's period dress and a Town Cryer also dressed in period costume. At one pm exactly, every Thursday the Town Cryer yells, "hear, ye, hear, ye" and a cannon is fired. Mandy knew someone who could put their plan together and so this one Thursday Jason and Julie were standing around when the Town Cryer yelled "Hear ye, hear ye, we have a special announcement". As luck has it, a reporter for a magazine was also there. She took some film which I later saw. Mandy had someone taking photos. Jason dropped down on one knee and asked Julie to marry him, in front of everybody. Julie was certainly surprised and took, it seemed like ages for her to answer, she said "YES" thankfully. He was over the moon and couldn't stop talking about it. It did present another problem. They weren't going to get married for a year, so it gave us enough time. Mark would need to move out of Jason's home. This had been Mark's home too for quite a few years, but he would have definitely been a third wheel, he often got Julie upset. Mark doesn't like change, so this was not going to be easy. He was going to be feeling like the outsider again.

Jeff and I decided to buy a house not far from Jason, so that Mark could be close by, and we could stay with him as often as possible until he found his way. It was during this time that Mark was becoming lonely and had no one close to be near, except us. Jason while close was pre-occupied. Mark felt he was losing his brother and being pushed out of his home. We looked at many homes and found one we wanted Mark to have a look at. It was the right price and Mark loved it. We involved him as much as possible e.g., what room did he want for his bedroom, where did he want the lounge to be, etc. He would need a new fridge; he would need to come and choose.

Well, all was in order and only one thing left to do before the wedding, Mark to leave. We thought it best he would go there only one or two nights there a week and we would also stay with him until he felt more comfortable. He was sad and lonely and pushed away. He finally was to move, and Jeff and I stayed with him for a few months and gradually went to our home back and forth. Carers were also very helpful in Mark coming to terms with his new life and being around for talks and concerns he might have. One in particular, Annie, is a God send. She still is, and Mark calls her his second mother, though when he said "these are my two mothers" in a shop recently, I had to explain that we weren't together, that Annie was like a second mum and a wonderful carer for Mark.

Julie decided to move in with Jason as the wedding was not far away. I thought it was a good idea to get used to each other. It was a good idea to find out what their needs would be when

Julie got her NDIS funding. Julie had concerns for her dad living alone. Her brother, Craig, although living a long way away came and supported his dad as much as possible. After the wedding their dad decided he would be best living closer to Craig and family. This was a relief for Julie not to worry.

Julie hadn't received NDIS funding. She had tried but she had limited understanding of what was required and kept getting stumbling blocks. The main stumbling block was her diagnosis. Her previous paperwork concerning her diagnosis when she was young had been lost and not recoverable. To make an appointment with a specialist and see them for diagnosis could take a very long time. Now she had recently been in hospital, and they had a diagnosis written on her paperwork, that of Cerebral Palsy. However, the paperwork was still in the hospital. She came with me so we could retrieve it. They made her pay $40 through freedom of information to get that paperwork. I thought it should have been hers anyway; but now we were cooking. I arranged an Occupational Therapist, for a report. All was good, now to submit it all for NDIS funding. We had an interview with the governing body, NDIA. She was very helpful and caring and she made Julie feel comfortable. All was on track, and she soon got her funding. Now for the best use of her money, we went through the different services as Julie had only one idea, one service, but I felt that this service could not help her as much because of her complex needs. We covered every angle and eventually Julie decided to have a support agency, Fraser Coast Family Networks and Annie. She had gotten to know Fraser Coast Family Networks and Annie through their supports with Jason. I was relieved and they could help with daily living skills and housework, cooking and exercise.

Now the date was set for their marriage. We did have to change it as arrangements couldn't work for one reason or another so now the date had to be set and plans had to be made. Julie's step-mother had died, as had her mother. Her brother lived in Emerald, some 10 hours away. Her father is incapacitated, and money was short. This left us with me and a lot of innovations from everyone. Mandy said the Brolga would be a nice place to have a wedding and Mandy had a lot of contacts. It was a lovely place to have a wedding, looking out, right onto the Mary River. We had the back patio, and the Brolga also threw in the seating for us to use. It had a stage area where the wedding could be held with people seated there while the ceremony took place. It was undercover so if it rained, it wouldn't matter. Julie and Jason both agreed, this was the place. The Brolga it was. They picked a date that was suitable to the Brolga and to them. Best of all, the Brolga could take care of the catering and flowers too. Thank God for Laurence who worked at the Brolga. He was so obliging and couldn't do enough for us. He also had the contacts and gave us a list of food and prices. They decided to have finger food as the wedding was to be at 1 o'clock. We thought this best because out of towners could get a motel room a couple of meters from the Brolga and have tea and settle in for the night. And Laurence was a florist in a previous life and he offered to do the fresh flowers for us. The Brolga had some dried arrangements too which he organised for us to borrow for the day, so this was teeing up really well. He also teed up volunteers for the day to serve us food and drinks. He thought of everything. We are so thankful. Thank you, Laurence. It would also be less expensive for us, but still beautiful. We organised a date which we changed again later. The date also had to suit the celebrant. Nothing was too much trouble for the Brolga. The invitations were to be sent. We asked Mark to come up with some designs for the invitations. Now to chop down the invitation list! Anyway, I managed to talk Jason and Julie into halving the guest list as we wouldn't be able to have it at the Brolga if there were too many people. They obliged and it was all organised, and invitations were sent. Now Maryborough is not a large town, so the next step was a wedding dress. Julie is a large girl, and it was difficult finding a dress in Maryborough in her size. We looked everywhere in opportunity shops, and on line. Nothing that fitted her. This was also the time of Covid so there were shops closed. Luckily a carer, Annie, had seen a beautiful lacey blouse that fitted Julie, so Julie bought it months earlier. We had options, we all still looked for a dress but if it wasn't going to be, then a skirt would be another option. There just weren't any dresses in her size on line. We scurried through opportunity shops and then there was this beautiful material, and yards of it in an opportunity shop. It was this gold silky material and what looked like brand-new tablecloths, 5 of them. Time was getting on, we hadn't seen anything, Julie liked the material, so we bought the tablecloths for $28. But we couldn't find a dressmaker after a few enquiries, so I took the plunge and I'd make it myself. Julie decided a flared skirt would be best that went down just past her knees as she didn't want to get caught up in it when she walked. It would also cover her curves appropriately. We just had an elastic waist and it would be comfortable for her. I organised for her hair and makeup to be done and her sister-in-law wanted to pay for it. When it was done, she did look absolutely lovely.

Jason had asked Mark to be his best man, much to Mark's delight. Annie had suits that her father had. They fitted the lads, except for a few minor adjustments. I made little handkerchiefs the same as the bride's skirt for their pockets on their suits. It was all shaping up. We went on a colour scheme for their shirts. They sure looked handsome.

There was only one thing left to do. A Hens night and a Bucks night. Us girls had a lovely night at the house while we did some belly dancing and, as Annie had some experience in this, she bought some garments and music to suit. Annie can certainly swing those hips, and the rest of us had fun trying!

I can't talk much about the buck's night because I wasn't there. Jason doesn't like a lot of people around him, so it was a quiet one with just a few people, or so they say. I did hear one of them say, "mum's the word"!

Jason then slept over at Mark's house as tradition has it, the groom can't see his bride the night before the wedding.

The big day came, and Julie had many relatives there who had travelled a long way. Both Julie and Jason had friends there and a couple of carers who were always going beyond their call of duty, both of them. This was just lovely for the bride and groom. Everything seemed to be going like clockwork. Now I had the music organised, I just had to put my iPod on with it having Bluetooth to a speaker. I had the bridal chorus or wedding march to play when she came down the pathway. What I didn't realise as I was running out to the front to see when she was coming, the Bluetooth disconnected. When she finally did come down the pathway, I was in a pickle. I finally got the iPod to work with the speaker, only to have the chorus of "Build me up Buttercup" being sung on my iPod. Damn, now I was really trying to stop it! Jill who had been our next-door neighbour for many, many years started to giggle. I never did see Julie walk down the aisle; I just had my head down the whole time. When I finally stopped it, it was too late, Julie was in front of the Celebrant. I should have given that job to one of the grandkids! I was very red faced but everything else went to plan. As the ceremony progressed Jason became emotional as he said, "I do". He has such a good heart!

Julie and Jason spent some time with Julie's out of town relatives. Jason and Julie spent the night in a Maryborough hotel next to where they had tea. The next morning, we had organised a honeymoon. We booked a place at Hervey Bay (about half hour away). Annie took them down and made sure they had meals planned and some walks, if they wanted to that is! Annie went down daily to ensure they were able to go out to places they'd never been and get anything they needed. Unfortunately, some activities were closed because of Covid. I'm pretty sure they still enjoyed themselves!

CHAPTER 8

Vulnerabilities

There was a sad occurrence that happened not so long ago in Jason's life. As mentioned, Jason had some friendships that were long lasting. One of those was Ben. Ben always stood by Jason, took him fishing, spending time with him, looking out for him. Ben passed away very young and while it isn't my place to say what caused his death, it is my place to say Jason hurt really badly. He could not come to terms that his mate had gone. The carers were just a God send. He continually got upset about it and he spoke about Ben often. Even though years have passed since then, Annie often takes Jason out to the cemetery when he wants, where he finds solace in talking to Ben.

Many years earlier Jeff's dad had died. Jason with his father was going to be a pallbearer. It was difficult because Jason is shorter than the other pallbearers. But I'm sure that Jeff's deceased dad would have had a smile on his face as the pallbearers and Jason were carrying him to his grave site and Jason said in a very loud voice' "he's heavy, isn't he?" Jeff didn't know whether to laugh or cry!

A vulnerable perspective for Mark is knowing that he is adopted. This sometimes has made him feel different or on the outer with the family. He has many coping and problem-solving strategies as you have seen. Not always the way I would have worked things out, but never the less he tries. It is hard for him not to be impulsive and think of consequences ahead of time. He sees something and wants it and goes for it, -- and then come the consequences! His latest innovation was wanting to move to San Francisco. I'm not sure what his fascination for San Francisco was except for the name of a song. But he became fascinated about going. He researched San Francisco and researched it. He stated that he could live there and get a job as a waiter, and everything you want is there. Now we know everyone has day dreams, but Mark was pricing tickets to fly to San Francisco. He looked up available jobs and he was sure he would find a place to live too. I showed him some photos of the homeless living on the streets and that he could be one of them. I told him it is very hard to get a job and you don't get a pension over there. For one job there is probably 100 other people going for it. Then they become homeless. I said there's nothing wrong with planning a holiday and have me or someone to go with him. Mark still wanted to live there. He told Annie that he still wanted to go and he would like to adopt a little brown boy when he went over there. We later realised he wanted to give a home to a homeless child. The pictures I'd shown of the homeless, showed the people to be predominately black. He does have a good heart! He finally thought that mightn't be such a good idea, so he changed his ideas to wanting to go to New York to see Channing Tatum because he wanted to have a body like his. He wanted to go to Los Angeles to meet the Charmed cast, particularly Piper. He thought he could stay in their mystical house and start another series with him in the series. We told him that Piper was probably old now as the TV series had been going for a number of years. She can't age in the series even if the series is years old.

It made me think that maybe he spent too much time watching TV and on the internet. We had given him a lot of internet time on his phone, and he does have a vivid imagination. It seemed that when one movie star departed from his thoughts, with a lot of help from carers and me, a new one emerged. We don't always find out about these thoughts until well down the line.

He loved the movie stars and thought he would write to Jennifer Gardiner. He found her apparently. He told me "Mum, now I don't want you to get worried because I am so happy". "I'm getting married to Jennifer Gardiner". We talked and talked about this and there was no convincing him that it was a scammer. He said, "no mum, she told me she wanted to marry me when I asked her if she was a scammer. She showed me a photo of herself". Annie and I told him how they lie to get you to believe them. Now the worst bit of news was that this scammer needed to get Mark's identity papers supposedly so she could get the marriage license. Oh yes, Mark had happily sent his photo ID, his 18+ card, his bank account details, his address, his date of birth, his Medicare card. He said, "oh don't worry mum, she said she didn't need my Medicare card because they don't have Medicare in America".

So, I frantically had to get to work while Annie worked with him in the background trying hard to find out more and convince him it wasn't the movie star, Jennifer Gardiner. I called the police who couldn't do anything because a crime had not been committed --- yet. They advised me to go on line to Cybercrime and put in writing a report of the scam. I also filled out a report so that no loans could be taken out in Mark's name. This only lasts for 1 month and then you need to reapply. We explained to Mark that they could take out a small loan in his name, pay that back and then get even a bigger one. They make you think that they are somebody famous so you fall for their lies. They want your money. He is still very trusting of what they tell him on line. He doesn't think they are telling lies, no matter what we say. So, I worked one end, Annie and Julian (another carer) worked the other end. Hopefully we would get through. When the scammer called him "scum" because Mark hadn't given them the money or mobile phone yet (because he couldn't afford it), I thought he would then understand. I told him that a nice person doesn't do that, especially if they want you to buy them a mobile phone. His answer to that was, "but mum, I don't mind". He wants to make it up to them. We had a good discussion, but nothing was convincing Mark. Mark values what Tammy says as well. Tammy who is a valued friend and a coordinator of another service, said to him, "Mark in all the years I've known you, have I ever asked you for money"? He said "no". She said "friends don't do that to each other. I would never borrow from you". "These people are scammers".

I went to the bank who were very obliging. They knew Mark well as Mark had tried to open various accounts with them, oh yes, that's another story! I had given them many years back, the paperwork from QCAT to say that I was Administrator and guardian of Mark. They had set up an account that could not have purchases made on line and/or loans. I also ensured that Mark could not take money out of this account or mine!!!!!, we made another account which he had a weekly amount put in for his budget. He could do whatever he wanted with it but he had to buy his food with it. Then all his other bills are paid through another account. QCAT get a yearly report with all his statements. I tried to get another 18+ card for him but I couldn't without a police report number, which I did get later. However, this would not have helped as it turns out. He hadn't finished with the scammers yet!

Mark was not convinced, and he started to hide things from me, I'm the bad cop! Annie isn't! He found another couple of movie stars whom he fell prey to once again. This time he was opening other bank accounts in other banks, because he wanted to buy a mobile phone for one of the scammers. We had our work cut out for us yet again. I went around to ANZ and NAB banks because I was told he had accounts there. They did not approve of the certified copy paperwork I had for me continuing to be administrator and guardian. They wanted the original documentation when guardianship was first granted some 10 years ago. Mark has free reign on these accounts until I organise myself. That means he can send money, buy phones, etc. My assertive skills will now need to be reined in, because I mean business! I have come to realise that Mark has accounts at every bank in Maryborough. It won't be hard for the scammers to take out, or indeed, get Mark to take out loans and credit cards. This is a frightening new age. I'm afraid there was no choice, I had to limit Mark's ability to go online. I went to Telstra and as I was also on his account, I was able to stop his internet entirely, and ensure no texts or phone calls could be done internationally. He had previously that month sent 5 international SMS messages. They said that if any changes were to be made, it had to be passed by me. He could not do it on his own. I hate taking away privileges, but I had no choice. I told all the carers what I had done so they could keep a watchful eye. Mark took it well; -- too well -- and I felt he was up to something. He had been talking about a new phone that would be available in 3 months' time. He was sure he would get one and he was also sure he would get internet back again if he proved himself. I also went to Optus and explained the situation and proof of my administration. They said they would make sure he didn't get a phone or sim card from them. I know he can get internet at the Shopping Centre, but it is limiting for him. I still have to handle the banks, except for the Commonwealth as they had come to the party a long time ago, when there was only one bank Mark dealt with. Originally though, even when I had the paperwork, the Commonwealth bank felt Mark still had the right to take out all his money and spend it and unset everything I had set up. I rang QCAT and they said it was court ordered, they must abide. I went back to Commonwealth bank and eventually I won that. Those assertive skills do me proud!! However even when I had the paperwork, I have found the other banks are not so obliging, and since Mark has accounts in all of them, I have to really practice my assertive skills! The carers have kept him really busy as well, so he has limited opportunity.

Here I have to say, the carers are worth their weight in gold. Esther has been there for the long haul and for many years now she has taught the boys lots of practical daily skills, cooking, safety, hygiene and--- using the sewing machine. Mark really wanted to learn how to use the sewing machine. He wanted Esther to teach him, only thing was Esther didn't know how to use a sewing machine either. I taught her and a little with Mark. Esther did the rest. He found it difficult with straight lines but with Esther by his side, he did it. Many, many hours went into making a beautiful material bag for me for when I went into hospital. Esther is very good inspiring the lads to pick recipes that are made with nutritional food. If there aren't any vegetables in their chosen recipe, they just get snuck in there. One day the boys had prepared a meal. With Esther's help and patience, they painstakingly cooked. They planned and had invited over Jeff and I and our friends, Lynda and George. It was very special, and the boys were delighted to have dinner guests. Another time with the carer, Annie's help, Mark put on a morning tea and planned and invited Esther, Jeff and I, Jason and Julie, and of course, Annie. They had a tablecloth, beautiful cups and saucers, and homemade cake. Mark waited on us. There was lots of conversation and laughter. How special was that!

We have recently hired a new support worker, Julian who gives Jason activities so he can do the blokey things that he has been lacking in his life since his work at the piggery has finished. Julian has Mark picking pineapples, and coffee groundings which are thrown onto a garden. Mark now mows, with Julian's help, his own lawn too. Mark also has Annie who takes him to appointments, helps him cook and clean his house, budget and buy food with her help, and they get to have some nice activities, like going to the movies and taking their dogs to the dog park. Troy who is employed by an agency, takes Mark and Jason separately to the gym. Julian now has started his own business and has other workers all who are just great with the boys and care about them and what they're doing. Jason is building a pig pen and is going to help Julian pick the pigs. He will help feed them and all the helping participants will eventually --- bring home the bacon! Thanks to Julian, Jason has also ridden a ride on mower, driven a small backhoe with carer support, of course. The boys often have a barbeque with other participants and have a social get together. This is really important for them. They boil the billy and do lots of blokey things. Both boys couldn't be happier.

One thing though. Since Jason as gotten married, Mark feels a little lost even though Jason comes down on a Sunday and spends many hours with him playing games. Several times a week, Jason looks after Mark's dog when Mark goes out. Mark has a feeling of being on his own. He could do with a best buddy. My next venture is to see if someone can do the group thing regularly, fishing, bowling, camping, kayaking, barbeques, going out for dinner with the same like-minded small group, so friendships can be made and maintained. Mark in particular is crying out for this. My eyes are looking Julian's way for this venture!

I often have to play good cop, bad cop, with the carers. I come in and say how things need to be and explain why. Then the carers follow through with my requests. It makes it best for carers as they are only doing what is requested: still being 'on Mark's side' so to speak. He has very good rapport with them all and tells them lots of things he doesn't always tell me, but I have my ways! You know what, ---- I've earned my stripes!

Annie is like a second mum to Mark, and when Mark decided he wanted to be a model, Annie became the photographer and took a progression of photos just as if he was modelling. They are very good and he might follow this path yet. He looks great and plays the part well. He loves being in front of the camera. He loves to buy clothes. I spotted Annie and Mark in a local clothing store. Mark introduced us, to the assistant, as his two mothers. I quickly explained that we aren't together, Annie is a carer for Mark and I'm his mother!

As I said earlier, I didn't have the carers and the support or help from anyone back in those days, 40 odd years ago. It was a hard slog. Probably hardest on the boys' two sisters, Sarah and Amanda. They would often help out but it isn't fair on siblings and looking back, I regret some of the decisions I made. Quite a few years back now, I did get some support with community access from block funding with Fraser Coast Family Networks which was all that was available for the lads to access, before NDIS. It wasn't much but it gave me a break. I am now determined to set things in place, so that the boys can survive well when Jeff and I are gone. We won't live forever, and we may not be capable to support them when we are older. I certainly don't want to leave any burden with Sarah and Amanda, they have their own lives to lead, and it would be nice that when they went to see their brothers, it will be a social occasion and an exciting family time and not one of duty. The other side to that is, that the boys do have their own lives to lead, interesting, having their friendships, independence, confidence, empowerment and control of their own lives and family contacts. Not have family members to make all their decisions for them. They are vulnerable but things are set to give them the very best of quality in life with their safety and life skills paramount. And you know what, I have the very best carers supporting the lads and thereby supporting all of us, supporting me. It is because of this I am able to study, I am able to have the work I love, to have fun, to dance, to sing, to play my ukulele, to travel, to spend quality time with our lads and the rest of the family. Please don't think that this is any lack of concern on Jeff's part, this book is about my experiences and perspective as a mother of two lads with disabilities. Jeff has been my rock, my inspiration and been there to hold my hand when the chips are down. He has never wavered. Having said that, in my experience it is the mother who has the most impact shed on her life, the one who becomes available for meetings at the school, to organise the carers, to ensure appointments are met, to talk to the lads when their impulse or determination takes over, to understand their thoughts and aspirations, to nurture when things go wrong, to be assertive. Now we have carers who have taken a lot of that responsibility. I do have to keep on the ball however, I am after all, -- their mother.

Time Out

When we are old, (some people might think we are already there!), I want to look back and think we have done the best job we could, and our lads are the best people they can be. I'll look back on the funny times, the hardships, their love, and their values. I will look back and think we have done our very best and these guys are well worth it. They are so loving, so kind, so funny, real characters and -- independent. And do you know what? The strategies put in place allows Jeff and I to be free to do the things we want in life, knowing the lads are well cared for. Their lives are sorted well after we die. We couldn't have had a better investment in life. I couldn't be prouder of all of my children's accomplishments. Sarah and Amanda have been dedicated in following their life's paths too. They have matured into caring, loving parents themselves. It has been hard for them also because they did miss out on some parental time. We did our best! There will always be trials and tribulations, but there is always fun and laughter along the way. I am their mum forever. How I love all our children so much. What beautiful people they have become.

Now our lads have something to say in this book. Annie decided to make it like an interview. She sure is a bottler carer. The lads loved this and apparently Mark didn't want to stop talking, but I think we may have run out of paper.

So here are their conversations while talking to Annie: -

Jason's Stories
Annie asked Jason about the best thing that happened to him in his life...

Childhood
- Meeting Ben Freear and his family. We were good mates and we lived in Tiaro. We used to go camping and fishing.
- I climbed a real tall tree and I climbed back down. Mum and Dad cracked up. Mum was shocked I climbed a real tall tree. I never climbed a tree like that.

Adult
Working Life:
My first Boss gave me a job at the Pig Farm. His name is Michael Wilks. I hand fed the pigs and did hosing and cleaning the pens out. I cleaned the pigs and branded them to go on the truck the next day for the markets. Sometimes I had to get up at 4.30am to get there to start at 6. The night before I had to get my smoko ready, morning tea and lunch. Sometimes I would have to get up at 2.30am to get there earlier to help load the pigs to market. Sometime in wintertime it was so cold getting up early.

I loved the job and got paid for it. I own my own home from working at the piggery for 26 years. I got a steel cup for working there so long and a photo frame and some money, 800 or so dollars.

Funny Stories ...
- I had braces and used my teeth to get the bait off the hook and the hook got caught and I pulled it and ripped my braces out and I had wire sticking out of my mouth.

- Ben's sister Kirsten came near the dam at Mum & Dads place at Tiaro. They got some eels in the dam. Kirsten was in the dam, and I could feel the eels. I grabbed it and said Snake! Snake! and she started screaming and took off. Ben was cracked up laughing and I did too.
- I had a 3-wheeler motor bike. I would ride at the farm at our family house. Dad made it for me. It was heaps of fun and Dad made me a shed for my weights.
- My biggest thing in my life is I got married. I never got married before. It made me feel real happy. I had tears down my eyes. I got engaged first before I got married. I bought an engagement ring and proposed to Julie at the park. We got married at the Wharf St next to the river.

On the day I saw Julie have tears in her eyes and she said, "yes, yes, yes, I will marry you".

My sister Amanda had tears in her eyes, and she said, "it was so sweet you made me cry".

- We got a furry baby, a king Charles cavalier cocker spaniel. His name is Toby T-Rex Charnock.

Julie choose Toby and me, I choose T-Rex for Tyrannosaurus Rex from Jurassic Park.

Q. If you could be anyone in the world, who would you be?
- I would be like Arnold Schwarzenegger because I want to get big like him and become like him and make a lot of money. My Idol is Arnie.
- I like Bruce Lee too. I like his fighting and his moves. He is the master of Martial Arts. I did Karate a couple of years ago. I was black belt.

Hobbies
- Going to the gym.
- Collecting DVD sets
- Dinosaur documentaries

- Jurassic Park & Jurassic World
- Shark DVDs
- Ten Pin Bowling every Friday night
- I love my walking.
- I lost 30 kilos in 3 years by eating healthier and eating smaller portions.
- Fishing & Camping

Q. My favourite TV Show…. is Home & Away
- I also like to watch Autopsy USA about Bruce Lee and Patrick Swayze and how they died.
- I also like scary movies like blood and gore. The scariest are the 18+ ones. The scariest was Freddie Kruger and Friday the 13th.

Mark's Stories
My Childhood
When I was a kid and I was adopted and mum and dad accept who I am and make the perfect family together. My real biological parents were living at the gold coast and reason they don't accept me is that I got a disability and they can't accept that and I can't give them that. I was born in the Southport hospital. I'm still looking for them and my parents tell me they love me and support me.

Then I had flashbacks of when I was born and when I was at the Sports Club - about what time I was born. I tried to see the time but some people blocking the time (in the hospital).

Jason was 13, mum and dad watched me when I was a kid and mum wanted to call me Kurt and I crawl on the floor and no one catch me and Jason said, "come here you little rascal".

School…
Mum almost take me to Riverside school and then my godparents told mum that another State high school is the best

school ever and she put her foot down. I was under SEU Special Education Unit, and I got the best teacher – Michael Bates. Then he got a son called Justin bates and I get along with him so good. Then Michael Bates died from a stroke, and I felt pain and didn't eat anything.

All the subjects I get D in hospitality and English. A in science. B in TAFE.

From Tiaro state school I went to, I was in in grade 7 and was Good in writing, good in German.

Learn advance of spelling and I like to spell and write neatly.

(Annie's Story re writing skills…Mark filled in his forms at the Hearing Clinic. When he gave the forms to the receptionist – she went WOW. Mark is such a good writer. He can write better than most people she has seen fill in their forms.)

Mark can remember his Centrelink number and Chemist membership number and often surprises people with his ability to remember long numbers that others can't remember…and Mark would like to add that Jason is good at remembering birthdays and numbers.

According to Mark: -
- I am the 4th kid in this family and my parents always spoil me a lot about everything. And when I was a little kid, I was a bit annoying to Amanda.
- Gavin Derek died of a heart attack, and I was really close to him.

The Best job I ever had…
- Tasty Restaurant… I was really good and everyone pleased about my skills. I take their order I serve them. I gave the order to the chef for their meals. I order their drinks. I was their waiter. A very absolutely good waiter.
- After that I was delivering hot drinks then I burned myself on my stomach.

- At the farmhouse I was cooking something on the stove and I burned my stomach and my sister Amanda was there and look after me.

FUNNY Stories…
- The funny part when mum was working at the piggery and then my 2 sister say, "Mum's home", then we had to put a peg on the nose because we don't want to smell it, it was disgusting.
- Mum said to my 2 sisters, she said, who's using a dirty teaspoon, just lick it and put it in the sugar.
- (Mum here. How that story actually went was that Amanda, when really little, put a dirty teaspoon in the sugar bowl. Sarah exclaimed, "Mandy, don't put that dirty teaspoon in the sugar bowl. Lick it first!")
- Mum had this dog, Tiny, both sisters went to school then Mum make a castle cake with icing on top with smarties for   Amanda's birthday. Mum went to pick the kids up from school and then after that Tiny got the castle cake and bring in downstairs under the house and eat it all up all over her face. And then she said (Tiny) don't look at me I never done it and all the cream was on her face.

Hobbies
- First class Cooking – it's fantastic, its classic and its good
- Spending time with Support Carers
- Snap fitness Gym
- Meeting people and spending time with Friends
- Lunch out
- Going to the movies at Hervey Bay Boat Club – Its bigger. Its better
- Watching TV shows and learning history on TV with Annie

- Sometimes I like to alone at home doing my own thing – having a beer, eating popcorn, eating McFlurries, organising my dinner, organise my clothes for Monday to Saturday, fold my pants in the cupboard.
- Spending time with Jason
- Organising a special occasion/event like Morning tea on ANZAC DAY with family or friends.
- I like to play a bit of tennis

My favourite TV Shows…
- Two Broke Girls, then MOM – "Show me what you got"
- Neighbours, Home & Away and The Bold and the Beautiful
- I like Comedy – Who's the Boss….Mona I like, she twists the words around!
-

Movies…
- The best movie ever will be…(looong pause……) The Mummy
- Electra, she's kick arse, dare devil – Jennifer Garner
- Crazy Ex-girlfriend – Rachel Blomms… she sings everything in her mind
- I like musicals and IP Man episodes online,
- Underworld with Kate Beckinsale
- Resident Evil
- Child Play
- Witchcraft – I like scary movies too

GOALS:
- To have a six pack on my body and big arm and big legs.
- Modelling – that's my favourite thing to do
- Gym
- Get healthy – protein drink, shake and juice

- Making my own tv show. Tv show about brotherhood and fatherhood, series episode.
- Chinese fighting
- JW
- I'd love to do thanksgiving every, once a month. It's about, it's a traditional way to share the love with the family. I saw it on the internet with Martha Stewart. She is a very inspiring woman to express her feelings to cook.
- I'd like to make my own coffee van
- I would like to get married with kids and the perfect dream wedding.

Loneliness
- I feel a little alone every day but I'm not alone with Rosa Lee Charnock (the dog). She sleeps up on my bed.
- I get emotionally when I'm with people around me. When it's too crowded I don't want to stay there too long.
- I get emotionally when I look and there is babies around.
- I get a new family, they're like a new family. New life, new family, they get me a lot and they show me how to be a part of them.

Q. How do you deal with stress….
- My advice would be to write everything down in a journal book.
- Cook
- Watch tv
- Play on mobile phone.
- Read a book
- Lay on carpet, Play with the dog
- I want to thank mum personally for hiring people to work with me. And I want to follow my dreams to hire people

- to work with me and I can be their personal assistant and they can pay me.
- I love Christmas, having lunch and put effort on it and bring a dish. Food family, presents.
- My only thing disappointing to me is my birthday and my parents will be away and my sisters will be working. (Julie said I could have it at her place (((but that will be too much drama for me)))). OOOH
- I better take that part back – Julie will take it personally.
- I don't mind go out for lunch or dinner.

End of Conversations

Once More

And to that wonderful person who both inspired me and gave me the commitment to write this book. Who made sure I wrote this book.

Desiree: ---- I have finished the book!! Finally!!

Post Script

Just a word. I have gone to the banks, where Mark has opened up all these accounts, to show them the Administrator forms. With a lot of effort, I think I have it covered. All the banks have different criteria, and it needs to go to their legal team or they need to enquire to higher up the ladder as they don't have many administrator requests. It seems it will be all sorted, - soon.

About the scammers who are pretending to be actors and actresses. Unfortunately, I had to turn off Mark's internet. However, he can still use the internet when he goes to the local mall. That makes it time limited. Even though I don't want him to talk to them, Mark continually and annoyingly chats to the scammers when he is at the mall. He doesn't have money to give them or send overseas. He tells them he wants to continue their friendship and that they are special to him. (He thought Jennifer Gardiner wanted to marry him). He just wants to talk to someone, but at least it isn't at night now, when the scammers are most active. I'm sure he was on their speed dial but now the tables have turned. They have become frustrated and asked him to f*** off. One scammer pleaded "why are you doing this to me?" Talk about reversed rolls!

We decided that Mark needs a trusted pen pal or two. He now has a past carer who has become his pen pal. She has put boundaries in place for her own mental health. I know that Mark will adhere to these rules as he doesn't want to lose her. I'll be looking for a few more pen pals now.

ABOUT THE AUTHOR

I have a full and interesting life with my husband Jeff and our 4 children, Sarah, Jason, Amanda and Mark. The two lads have Down's Syndrome. I love to see all four children grown up into beautiful adults with families of their own. Because of my life's journey, I have become and indeed love working as a mental health social worker, now semi-retired. We have plans in place for the lads, so my husband and I are free to travel.

www.ingramcontent.com/pod-product-compliance
Lightning Source LLC
Chambersburg PA
CBHW050843160426
43192CB00011B/2130